SKYSCRAPER

GOING BEYOND YOUR LIMITS TO REACH GREATNESS

RAHFEAL C. GORDON

*To Chantel,
May the book take you higher! Let's continue to move higher in the years to come!
—Rahfeal*

Copyright © 2015 Rahfeal C. Gordon.

Edited by Lauren Thomas
Cover Picture taken by Baa-ith Nurri-deen
1st Project Assistant: Melissa Gutzmore
2nd Project Assistant: Asiah Lemon
3rd Project Assistant: Brenelle Tyus

All rights reserved. No part of this book may be reproduced, stored, or transmitted by any means—whether auditory, graphic, mechanical, or electronic—without written permission of both publisher and author, except in the case of brief excerpts used in critical articles and reviews. Unauthorized reproduction of any part of this work is illegal and is punishable by law.

ISBN: 978-1-6810-1018-2 (sc)
ISBN: 978-1-6810-1010-6 (hc)
ISBN: 978-1-6810-1009-0 (e)

Because of the dynamic nature of the Internet, any web addresses or links contained in this book may have changed since publication and may no longer be valid. The views expressed in this work are solely those of the author and do not necessarily reflect the views of the publisher, and the publisher hereby disclaims any responsibility for them.

Any people depicted in stock imagery provided by Thinkstock are models, and such images are being used for illustrative purposes only. Certain stock imagery © Thinkstock.

Rev. date: 05/16/2016

Dedication

This book is dedication to my beautiful
grandmother Oreleen Warren.
Thank you for being a strong pillar in my life.
Thank you for being a foundation for me
to stand as tall as a Skyscraper.
For I know God loves me so much that he
blessed me with a grandmother like you.

Contents

Introduction	xi
Role Model vs. Superhero	1
The Tree of Life	5
Two Monks by the River	12
Be Like the River	17
A Promise by the Docks	19
Three Stages of Transformation	23
Look Harder Into Your Vision	28
Chicken and the Hawk	38
Light Language	48
We live not by our words alone but also by their meaning.	50
D3=F Philosophy	62
The Equation To Greatness	64
Creating Quantum Leaps in your Life	82
RahGor K-Studies to Help You Reach Your Greatness	86
Rahfeal Gordon's 21 Days of Greatness Journey Activity	115

THE STORY BEHIND THE TITLE SKYSCRAPER

After completing the rough draft of this book, I began thinking about a title. I didn't want just any title but wanted something that resonated with my readers to provoke an even deeper connection. I know that creativity cannot be forced, and so I released myself of the pressure to think constantly about the title of the book. Simply, I advised myself, "When it comes, I will know by the way it makes me feel."

One day, while heading into New York City by bus, I received a phone call from my grandmother. She asked me how things were going and how the book process was treating me. During our conversation my grandmother stated how proud she was of what I was doing and who I've become. She poured into me. She inspired me. She motivated me. She gave me the energy I needed to keep going.

She ended our phone conversation by saying, "Rahfeal, you are my skyscraper and I am your foundation. I am here to make sure your stand tall and go as high as the heavens. Keep rising, my skyscraper. I love you."

After the call, I felt goosebumps all over my body. I thought, "Thank you God for my grandmother." As I looked out the window, I knew. Quietly I said to myself, "Skyscraper... that will be the title of the book."

Introduction

My method to achieving greatness is simple. (1) Work smart. (2) Work hard. You can read all the books you want and study whoever is considered the greatest of all greats in the land. Whether in a book or hearing the words straight out of the mouth of someone great, the message remains the same: the most rewarding road to take when tapping into and unleashing your true potential in the world is the work you put into your vision.

I study my butt off. No, really! I study my BUTT off to achieve the vision I have for myself. My vision does not include failure therefore I do not allow myself the space to be lax on projects or situations I know I have the capability of dominating. Your work ethic should be so imperative that if your vision had a heart, your work ethic would be its beat. No work ethic, no heartbeat, your life has flat lined at the hand of mediocrity. Sounds harsh, right? Truth and reality can be harsh. You want to know what it takes to be great? Lesson #1: Greatness is not for the faint of heart. There is no room in greatness for you to be afraid. You are reading this book because you want to be equipped with all the right tools to conquer your fears and see the world from your mountaintop. Am I right? Then keep reading, my friend!

"You will give the people an ideal to strive towards. They will rest behind you, they will stumble, they will fall. But in time they will join you in the sun. In time, you will help them accomplish wonders."

- Russell Crowe, *Man of Steel*

Role Model vs. Superhero

"You and I... with what we do... what's at stake... we can't fail. Others don't understand, but even if it's... impossible, we still have to succeed."

– Bruce Wayne

Over the past five years, I have been labeled a role model. In the beginning, I was honored, I accepted this label and tried my best to live up to its characteristics. But today, I have outgrown it. I no longer believe in it, and I am no longer attached to it. Being a role model is a box much too small for my greatness, and so I've freed myself from it.

Let's explore the actual definition.

Role: The function assumed or part played by a person or thing in a particular situation.

Model: A three-dimensional representation of a person or thing; of a proposed structure, typically on a smaller scale than the original.

So essentially, you could say that a role model is an actor, a performer. They are what society has programmed people into believing they should imitate. When society gives such a title, they also attach a required set of standards that role models must follow. There are only two sides to the role model spectrum; a "good" role model or a "bad" role model. By accepting either of these labels, you are indirectly encouraging people to accept giving up their true selves all in the name of imitating you. This is the only power a role model can possess. It is a regulated power given to whom the individuals have labeled.. A role model's power is limited, confined and only determined by the approval of someone else. As a role model, you allow people to pick and choose what side you are on. In other words, there is a zero tolerance rule for human error.

People can see a person who is doing well for him or herself and say, "_____ is a GREAT role model." But the moment that person does/says/believes in something not in accordance with the behavior of a role model, there is an immediate switch. NOW you will hear, "_____ is not a good role model. He or she is not a good example for the youth or society." The pedestal is immediately lowered. It's very interesting because regardless of whether a person is in a good or bad place in their personal life, society says that they are still a role model. They have an obligation to ignore or hide their shortcomings, imperfections, personal struggles and to perform in a way that should be emulated. Being (or acting like) a role model can lead a person in the right or wrong direction. We all know individuals that are good or bad influences and serve as role models within the world.

Furthermore, I realized that role models do not use their godly (inner) power with pure intensity because of the limitations of role model standards. Using their higher power could put them on the opposite side of the role model team, either good or bad. In that respect, role models may not realize that they are in fact brainwashing their followers. In contrast, superheroes wash the brain of all those that come into their presence.

Super: Very good or pleasant.

Hero: A person who is admired for their courage or noble qualities.

Superheroes are real. Superheroes don't wear capes and fly but they are all over the world. They are not on display like mannequins in store windows but we come into contact with them every day. They are the people who say something as simple as "Good morning" and it sticks with us throughout the day. They are the people who have a vision of a better world and have made it their life's purpose. They recognize their godly powers and use them for the protection and enhancement of community and mankind. They do not feel the need to conform or imitate anyone because they understand that they are THE ONE. They are the chosen ones.

Superheroes go against the grain. They don't embrace the opinions of mere men because they know who they are. They determine what they can and can't do. They understand the path they take is their own personal journey and is not forced on them by anyone's standards. They are special people who are crucified daily by the same people they love and aim to protect within society. And even though they may be blamed as the cause of mankind's problem, superheroes continue to serve, sacrifice, and save. Superheroes are very much so aware of their weaknesses and will seek out its source to eliminate the root. A superhero will not allow a weakness or fear to be a hindrance on their path of greatness.

These extraordinary beings are humble and walk within the world but are not of the world. They tend to seek complete solitude for meditation, deep thought, and recharging of their powers. Likewise, they seem to draw inspiration from memories of the past and words from the wise in order to make heavy decisions that they know will have an impact on their journey. But they are solely concerned about the affect those decisions will have on humanity.

Superheroes give hope and inspiration. They are good-hearted individuals. Some superheroes discover who they are early in life while others accept their identity in later years. Superheroes cannot be imitated. They cannot be role models because the level at which they operate cannot be computed by mere men. Men cannot choose who can be a superhero as is the case with role models. Instead, superheroes are chosen by a higher power.

To recognize a superhero in the present and future, first you must study the superheroes of the past. Mother Teresa. Gandhi. Martin Luther King, Jr. Moses. Jesus. The Dalai Lama. Nelson Mandela. See the pattern? All followed their own individual paths, went against what man said they "should" do, and stood firm in their beliefs that the world could be made a better place by following their example. Too many people use titles and material things to claim the position as superheroes. But covering themselves with these frivolous things are only to hide their fear. They are scared to think, build, fly, share, leave behind, and be completely free to just BE.

Inventory check: Are you a role model or are you a superhero? Choose wisely and do the work.

The Tree of Life

Be a Tree of Life

We are all trees. We are all connected to the universe through our roots. Every day we have the opportunity to grow tall and strong to provide the best fruits that a tree can bear. We should continuously inventory check ourselves to be certain that we are truly growing and tapping into our true and highest potential.

The Root

All trees began at the root. The root is the beginning. It is where we find out why foundations fell and how they became so strong. The root is where the story begins. It is attached to the Alpha and will give the testimony at the Omega

Inventory check: All roots are connected to a source. What source are your roots connected to? Where do your roots sprout? What do you reference when you explain why you grew or fell? Who do you quote? Who does your root mimic and reflect when you are pushing to stand tall and individually over the rainforests you come in contact with? Roots tell a story before you tell yours. Roots tell the truth even when your leaves try to make your lies colorful.

The Environment

We are a direct reflection of our environment. We did not have a choice where we wanted to be when we were seeds. We were planted by the divine hands of the universe (which I call God). As we began to take root and were deeply implanted in the soil we were placed in, we began to move upward in our environment. As we began to move upward, our particular environment recognized us and gave attention to see what type of tree we may grow into.

Our environments, all environments, have the capability to develop all kinds of trees. The question is, what type of tree does your environment accept and nurture? How many trees are planted in your environment but never grow tall, strong and bear fruit to sustain life? As a tree of life, it is your duty to make sure your roots are firmly planted in the right soil within an environment. You want to make sure all living things that surround you allow you to grow as tall as you are able to. Likewise, you want to make sure that the living things that surround you are able to benefit from your roots. It will be impossible for this to happen if your environment doesn't care for trees of your type.

Inventory check: If you feel that the environment that you are in isn't nurturing your tree, you must pick up and leave. There cannot be any hesitation when making this decision because the longer you wait to move, the easier it will be for you to dry out and die. Beware. If the environment you are in doesn't nurture trees of your type, it will swiftly, without any hesitation, cut you down and replace your position.

The Inhabitants

Trees that are full of life are able to house other lives as well. Many things want/need to live in the tree when it is fully grown. These things know how important a tree of life is within the world. A tree holds many keys to the doors of the living. As fully vibrant trees all over the world, we must always be at attention to the things we allow to dwell within and around us.

A tree is shelter. A tree is a food producer. A tree is a life bearer. A tree is the emotion of an environment. A tree is the reader of the seasons. I am a tree. You are a tree. As trees, we must preserve ourselves. Every branch, every leaf, every seed that will produce new life. We are responsible for the reproduction of magnificent trees in the world. Always remember, respect and recreate your tree in the world.

Inventory check: Who do you allow to stay connected to you on a daily basis? Who do you allow to inhabit your thoughts periodically? Are they nurturing the figure of your tree? Will they protect your tree from those who may do it harm? As trees, you want LIFE (not death) to dwell within and all around you. Be certain that they are assisting your tree in producing more life energy. There is no good in letting all things inhabit every part of your life.

The Pruning

Pruning is a continual duty and responsibility that we all have to take on. Those who don't prune consistently and/or periodically will grow wild and allow all types of inhabitants to live within it. You must not do so. It will stunt your growth. It will weaken your branches that are still maturing. It will drain all the energy you possess in your trunk.

Inventory check: Who do you allow to prune your tree? We all need pruning so that we don't look or grow out all wild. There are many landscapers who are willing to prune your tree, but not every one of them are skilled enough to do so. You must make sure to be thorough in choosing the right landscaper. You don't want someone to help you grow better, bear fruit better or be more of an attractive tree yet they never had the spirit or skill to assist in your elevation.

The Seasons

Seasons are the process to determine if a tree is strong or weak. It's within these seasons of change that will allow all living things in the forest know if a tree has strong and deep roots or if it is too weak to survive the harsh seasons. Seasons test all existing things in the universe to see if it deserves life or death.

We all have to deal with the seasons as they change over. As a person who is developing their light within, you must be excited about all seasons. Not just one. Not just your favorite. You must be willing to accept what will die in the winters as well as what will be born in the springs. You must be willing to be the child who gets excited to play in the snow rather than the adult who complains about the snowstorm. Growth exists in all seasons.

As a tree of life, you have to be aware of the seasons. Your very existence depends on it. When you are not able to recognize the shift of weathers in your life, you are leaving yourself vulnerable and susceptible to be beaten down by storms and winds of force.

Inventory check: How does your tree holdup to the harsh and changing elements of the seasons? Can you sustain focus to grow when the seasons change?

Autumn

Autumn is the season of transition from summer to winter. In our personal lives, we must be aware of when we are going into our autumns. It is the sign of transition from summer into winter. For us, this is the sign that we are heading into our hardcore development stages. When this season is upon us, the nights come noticeably earlier, the temperature becomes cooler. Tree leaves change colors and shed in preparation for something new. These external changes are reflective of our internal season changes as well. Autumn is our preparation of growth to the next level in our lives.

Winter

Winter is the season of trials and tribulation. The winter season is the coldest season of the entire year. The axis of the Earth in the respective hemisphere is being oriented away from the Sun. When we talk about the season of winter within us, it is our faith and knowledge being tested at its maximum. Just like the earth season of winter, our days are shorter and nights are longer. Many people can't survive the harsh season of winter due to lack of preparation. All that we have done and gained through the other 3 seasons are put to the test to determine if we have what it takes to survive and thrive.

Spring

Spring is the season of rebirth, rejuvenation, renewal, resurrection and regrowth. Spring is our trophy for passing Winter's test. Once Spring has arrived, we know that the storms of the winter season have passed and we have survived through it. When we experience the season of Spring, it is a sign that we have faced our trials and tribulations with our faith and inner strength. All things anew show in the Spring. The trees show new leaves, the grass becomes greener, life flourishes on land and in seas. The days can hold up to 12 hours of pure sunlight. In the season of Spring, our light beams brighter and longer. We are made stronger and have given birth to new ideas and views of seeing the world.

However, even though the Spring give us peace of mind about the storms we've faced, we have to be aware that we are still developing and gaining our strength back from battling our inner harsh winters. During the Spring, occasional unstable weather may occur when warm air begins to invade from lower latitudes while cold air is still pushing from the Polar region. This is normal on earth and just as well within ourselves. Even though we have come out of one season and begin to reap the blessings of going through the Winter season, we have to understand how to properly manage our new strength, wisdom, knowledge, blessings and all the new light we've acquired. It can take the entire season to get acquainted with your new self, but that's what Spring is all about.

Summer

Summer is the season of completion. The summer season has the longest days and the shortest nights. Summer makes you feel like there are no worries, no struggles. Summer is our celebration for getting through all the other seasons. You reap all your blessings in this season. Many people find this a great time to go on vacation, make extra time to see family in far off lands, and even experience some new things that they couldn't in the other three seasons. The season of summer is the season of blessings and light.

The Bearing of Fruit

The tree of life will produce fruit for all those within the environment and the inhabitants that are connected to it. The fruit you bear will tell those around you where your roots are planted.

From the Holy Bible, Matthew 12:33 states, "Make a tree good and its fruit will be good, or make a tree bad and its fruit will be bad, for a tree is recognized by its fruit." What does your tree bear? In the years of my development, I wasn't at the stage of bearing fruit. I was still trying to understand my bark, my environment, and my seasons. Not all trees bear fruit (life). There are several reasons for this. It could be due to bad roots, lack of nurturing (water) or constant harm done to it by those who inhabit the tree or around it (i.e. termites).

Bearing fruit is the highest blessing a tree can give and receive. Trees are a symbol of life. Stories from all over the world talk about moments that happen around, on and within a tree. Bearing fruit allows you to feed other living things that need help in their growth and development. The fruit you bear makes you a resource and an asset to the environment.

Inventory check: Examine your tree, your soil, and the environment which you are grounded in. Be certain that you are bearing good fruit. If you bear bad or no fruit, it leaves you alone. No one wants to be near you. Children will be warned not to play around you. People who are dying that needed your fruit will wither away. What is the fruit that you bear? Do you give life or are you destroying life? You are an exact reflection of the fruit you bear.

Two Monks by the River

There were two monks, one old and one young. Each and every day both monks would leave their village to meditate and pray in the woods as it was as a part of the culture and tradition as monks. They would pray and meditate for hours. Afterwards, they would head back to their village before sunset.

As they headed back, they would come to a river that they would have to cross. It was called, "The River of Life" and named so because people would come there to fish, wash their clothes, bathe, and quench their thirst. Also, it was a place where wildlife would come to find food and quench their thirst as well.

Each time the two monks came to the river, there would be a different woman there. Each woman was truly beautiful in her own way. However, because they were monks, they were not allowed to touch or associate with these women regardless of their beauty. Therefore, each time they saw a woman, they would just turn their heads and proceed across the river to their village.

One day, the two monks were heading back to the village from their daily meditation in the woods and saw a pregnant woman at the waterfront. It seemed as though she was trying to cross the river but was having a difficult time because of her pregnant body.

The old monk said to the young monk, "I know you see her, but we must let her be. We must have no dealing with her. Let's stay on the path so that we arrive at our destination by sunset."

The young monk understood what he was being told, but a feeling came over him. A feeling he never felt before. A feeling of compassion. (The same thing that we all feel when we aim to be a light within the world.) He looked at the old monk who proceeded to put his left foot in the water. He turned and said to the old monk, "But why? She needs help. Are we not supposed to help when someone is in need? I am in a state of confusion right now elder."

The old monk pulled his left foot out the water, turned around and said, "It has to be like this. It has always been and it will always have to be." The young monk listened but still didn't understand why it must be like this. The old monk proceeded to place his foot back in the water and began to walk across the river. He assumed the young monk was following him as he normally would. But to his surprise, when he reached the other side of the river, the young monk was not beside him.

The young monk could not let this woman struggle across the water. So he went over to her and put this woman on his back and carried her across the water. When they arrived on the other side, the woman gave the young monk her highest praises and blessings over his life. She was so grateful for what he had done because she knew that it was against the monks' tradition. He smiled, bowed his head to her, and went on his way.

He saw the old monk in the distance waiting for him so he sprinted quickly towards him. He knew the old monk would be very upset with him, but he kept running towards him with a smile on his face. The old monk was very hurt and upset. They continued on their way but the old monk kept stopping and saying, "How could you do that? Why did you do that?" The young monk wasn't paying the old monk much attention and didn't realize how fast he was walking through the woods. When he turned, he noticed the old monk had fallen behind him and the sun was already beginning to set.

The young monk stopped and yelled out, "Elder. We must get back. The sun is setting. Our pace is becoming slow. We must get back." Usually, the elder is leading and giving the instructions and reminders. But this time around, it was the young monk. When the old monk caught up to the young monk, he again questioned, "Why did you? How could you?"

The young monk was so confused. He asked, "Elder, what do you mean? Why did I what? How could I what?" The old monk replied, "Why did you pick up that woman at the waterfront? How could you break the tradition of our ways?"

The young monk stood there in disbelief and with a sense of disappointment towards his elder. He replied, "Elder, I love you so much but, in this exact moment, you are thinking in the ways of those who are lost. You see, I picked that woman up and brought her across the river because she was in need of help. Once I completed my task, I left her there by the river. But I see you are still carrying her. And because of this, you are holding us both back from reaching the village by sunset.

Internal Grips

Most people tend to keep a tight grip on past issues and situations that have caused them pain. There are people who have a tight grip on grudges that were created years ago. If this is you, you must let it go. There is no need to allow something of the past to hinder you from fully experiencing your "right now." In the story I just shared, notice how the young monk stated how he loved the old monk. Notice he pointed out to the old monk that because his focus was on what happened hours prior, they would not make it back to the village by sunset.

The grips you have on situations and past emotions can truly be toxic for healthy development in mind, body and spirit. You can't tell the Universe you want to be a light in the world and hold on to dark emotions or experiences. Release those grips. Release those grudges. Release those heartaches. Release those experiences that made you sad. Instead… Grip happy memories. Grip healthy ways of living. Grip the emotion of joy and the lifestyle of happiness. Remember, whatever you grip can either help you move forward or keep you stuck in a manner of backwards living.

When you don't release those internal grips, you set yourself up for destruction. You don't allow yourself to heal properly. Toxic emotions fester and overflow within and you become a ticking time bomb ready to explode. When you release your internal grips, you make room to hold onto and enjoy the new things that are sure to come into your life. These new blessings can come in the form of feelings of joy, healthy relationships, new belief system, great memories, new standards, new thought patterns, and even a new lifestyle. You have the opportunity to hold onto something different when you release yourself from the things that held you down, things that held you back. Give yourself permission to release yourself from toxic belief systems and begin to hold onto healthier ones. Give yourself permission to release the grip of the emotions of past hurt and begin to hold tight to the memories of conversations from people who helped you heal.

Here are some things to help you release internal grips:

- Do daily inventory checks of what makes you upset or gives you negative energy.
- Question why you have negative emotions towards an individual/situation. (You definitely want to get to the core of this.)
- Remind yourself of your end goal and why it is important to not waste time and energy on holding onto toxic emotions.
- Have a conversation with those who have changed for the better. Inquire about their methods and see if what they did would be a great method to use.

There are many ways to help you begin your release of those inner grips. Take it day by day but don't waste time. Start now with releasing. Start with one finger and next thing you know, your entire hand will be released and free to grab onto your new blessings.

Be Like the River

You must be like a river if you want your life and all that surrounds you to flourish. Rivers carry the source within its currents. You must be like a river if you want your environment to change and sustain during various seasons. Be aware of this in order for the ocean (universe) to constantly pour into you.

The Types of River

We all have the honor and blessing of choice in this world so there will always be decisions to make. As each day passes, we experience growth. Within that experience, there is always a choice, a fork on your path. There are two types of rivers in the world: a clean river and, of course, a polluted river. Daily, we have to choose what type of river we are going to be. You may have decided to be a clean river on Monday, but by Tuesday, your actions could reveal that you've actually decided to be the polluted river.

Clean rivers attract all types of living things to drink from its waters. It is the reason villages are established near it. Clean rivers preserve life as well as attract it. It helps to sustain life and assists in keeping all living things around it healthy. The waters are full of natural minerals and truly refreshing. Children yearn to play in the rivers and all beings want to bathe in it. Its currents can be gentle as a baby finger tap and as strong as a bear hug. But no matter the force of its currents, it is always well appreciated and needed.

In contrast, polluted rivers own waters that are dark and full of death. All living things that dare to consume of these waters eventually die. Its current is constantly rough and very self-damaging. Polluted rivers scare children and are rarely visited by their parents. This is not the type of river you want to project. It is harmful to your health and a surefire way of killing your spirit.

Inventory Check: There are two rivers in the world. Which one are you going to be each day?

A Promise by the Docks

There was once a man who prayed for a boat and a map that would lead him to his promise land. One day, all that he had asked for was granted unto him a hundredfold. He had everything he ever wished for and could have left the docks at any moment. He took pictures in the boat, hosted a big celebration party, and visited everyone he knew to talk about his blessings.

Day after day passed and people would still see him at the docks. The young man never sailed away. Days turned into weeks, weeks turned into years. The boat decayed and the map became so worn out that it was worthless. One day, a young boy walked up to the man, who was now old, and asked, "Mister, why do you sit at the dock every day? Why didn't you sail away like you always wanted?" The old man replied, "I didn't realize that I couldn't take everyone with me on my boat. I was too scared of my own adventure.

Now, I am an old man with the regret of not knowing what could have been. I feared that I would drown. I began to fear the sharks that I would encounter. I started to worry that I wouldn't want to come back here." The young boy felt sad for the old man and hugged him as tight as he could.

As the young boy hugged the old man, the old man said, "My dear boy never ever be scared of your promised land. When you receive your map, celebrate *while* sailing in your boat. It will get you through the rough waters. And always remember that your boat doesn't have the capacity to fit everyone. If you take heed to my words, you will see what I never saw. My ruins are now gifts of wisdom for you. Don't let them drown in a sea of regrets when you get older." As the young boy released his arm from the hug he created, he replied, "I promise."

Our Promise Land

We have all been given a gift. We were all chosen by something greater than ourselves. We were given **life**. Life is our promise land. All that we would like to experience in this lifetime, we can. It is with our lives that we can decide if we live in our own heaven or our own hell. We indirectly make a promise to our thoughts by the actions we are freely able to take in our lives. We are reflections of our thoughts in so many ways. Our thoughts are a promise that we make to our lives every day.

The Best Time

The best time to do anything will always be NOW. Every moment is the best time. Every second that is counted is the best time. Fear tends to have many people waste their best times away. People get complacent and comfortable with their current location because there is work attached to "the best time" to do something. Hesitation creates regret. Hesitation gives power to past issues and holds you back from truly reaching your greatness. Just as the sailor who never got on his boat.

It is important that you celebrate while on your boat. Enjoy your process more than your reward. There is so much to see when you are on your boat sailing towards a destination that is intended just for you. Be happy when you pick up winds and be happy when there aren't any. Relax, soak up the sun, wait and be prepared if the breeze comes again. There is no telling what could be on the island you are sailing to. You may have a better time on your boat than you would on the island. Every minute is the future of the past. Live in it to the fullest.

Mistakes to Learn

Learn from the mistakes of others. This will save you so much time and trouble. There will always be things that you will mess up, but that comes with anything in life. No one is perfect and we all have made the worst decisions with the best intentions in mind. Life can be chaotic and full of ruins, but that doesn't mean it's a bad thing. Experiences like this help to shape and transform us for something greater in life. But we have to be smart and make sure that we bypass as many storms and potholes as we can on our road to greatness.

> *"A friend took me to the most amazing place the other day. It's called the Augusteum. Octavian Augustus built it to house his remains. When the barbarians came, they trashed it along with everything else. The great Augustus, Rome's first true great emperor. How could he have imagined that Rome, the whole world as far as he was concerned, would be in ruins? It's one of the quietest, loneliest places in Rome. The city has grown up around it over the centuries. It feels like a precious wound, a heartbreak you won't let go of because it hurts too good. We all want things to stay the same. Settle for living in misery because we're afraid of change, of things crumbling to ruins. Then I looked at around to this place, at the chaos it has endured - the way it has been adapted, burned,*

pillaged and found a way to build itself back up again. And I was reassured, maybe my life hasn't been so chaotic, it's just the world that is, and the real trap is getting attached to any of it. Ruin is a gift. Ruin is the road to transformation."

- From the movie "Eat Pray Love."

Reflecting Your Environment

Our environment is the extension of our beliefs and standards in life. I'm not talking about a child or teenager; their direction and development is usually steered by parents, teachers, people they look up to. I'm specifically talking about you, the adult.

Our environment is the external picture of what we allow in our life and ways of living. The environment we choose is our thoughts' version of the Mona Lisa. Whether the environment is toxic or full of love, it is what we accept and attach ourselves to. Being a light in the world, you must make sure your environment is clean, organized, safe and welcoming for all people. Your environment should not give off an exclusive vibe where only a certain type of person is allowed. No. That's not love. And that's not beautiful. Your environment should be one of peace and authenticity. One that welcomes people to be who they are, no matter where their roots are planted.

Three Stages of Transformation

"As human beings; our greatness lies not so much in being able to remake the world... as in being able to remake ourselves."

– Gandhi

Being transformed is a 3-part process: chaos, ruin, and transformation. Throughout our lives, we go through these stages periodically because of the experiences and lessons we gain along our journey. I want to share with you these three stages in hope that you recognize them when going through your journeys.

Stage One: Chaos

I was doing some research on the term chaos and found some interesting things. Chaos is defined as complete disorder and confusion. This is something I knew. Simple and straight to the point. Then I stumbled across the term Chaos Theory, which is a field of study in mathematics. Chaos Theory has several applications in several disciplines including meteorology, physics, engineering, economics, biology, and philosophy.

As I dug deeper into this theory, I found another definition for chaos: When the present determines the future, but the approximate present does not approximately determine the future. Quite interesting, right? We all have encountered chaos before. If you have not, life will surely prepare some for you if you are claiming to be a light within this world. Chaos is just as necessary as peace. When change is upon you, things have to shift. Things will have to change internally and externally. This is what can cause friction on various levels in your life.

> "Then I looked around this place, at the chaos it has endured - the way it has been adapted, burned, pillaged and found a way to build itself back up again. And I was reassured, maybe my life hasn't been so chaotic, it's just the world that is, and the real trap is getting attached to any of it."
>
> -Eat Pray Love

When you are experiencing change, it can cause friction because you are attached to what has to be destroyed. As you grow, there will be some things you have to let go. These releases come in various forms: how you dress, materialistic items, relationships, social places, old habits, and even places of residence. Being attached to something that has to be destroyed is hard. You may have worked so hard to acquire some of these things. You may have had to sacrifice to own what now has to be destroyed or released. Enter: chaos.

There is also internal chaos. Living out a dream that someone else has placed on you can be chaotic when you're trying to conform and be someone you're not. Trying to keep up with other people who have already found themselves and realizing that you have not yet found yourself. This causes confusion. I remember when I was in college and I was so lost because I was listening to everyone telling me what I should be doing with my life. What type of major I should study. Where I should work. Where I should live. How to do this. And how to do that. It caused major chaos in my life. I needed a break. I needed to quiet the outside voices. I could hear these voices but was deaf to my own. This is how your light dims. This is how chaos runs rampant through your life with no remorse.

Staying attached to the ideals, expectations, and visions that other people have created for you is very unhealthy. You weren't created to be what someone else wants you to be. They haven't allowed their own voice a chance to be heard. Staying attached to material things is painful in the long run because all material things will be damaged and destroyed.

Stage Two: Ruin

After chaos, comes ruin. Ruins are proof that chaos has happened. It is the evidence that something or someone has gone through something heavy and powerful. A person can take on the form of ruin too. People walk around various environments as a "ruin." They show others that they could not survive the storms of chaos. A person who continues to abuse their body with drugs will eventually become a ruin. The person who didn't care for their health over the years eventually becomes a ruin. Ruins are the second stage of Transformation. It is a level that many people stay on because the chaos in their lives knocked them completely down. And these individuals feel it is best to stay there and not go through the pain of getting knocked down again in the near future. But remember: Although it may not always seem like it, "Ruin is a gift."

Stage Three: Transformation

Finally, after the chaos and ruins, there is transformation. Transformation is just as intense as the first stage (chaos). The reason is that there are shifts and changes constantly occurring. This is why, as I stated before, many people don't get past the second stage. It takes a lot of work and you are, in some sense, starting from scratch.

Transformation by definition is a thorough or dramatic change in form or appearance. Most times we tend to make a transformation due to something we experience externally or something that is affecting us internally. Just so you know, not all transformations are positive. Have you ever heard of a person who was such a great person but due to something happening in their life, they transformed into someone considered bad?

Transformation is a process that starts heavily in details. I'm talking about thought process, daily rituals and activities, the repetition of small duties. To allow your light to shine as bright as it can, you must be content with constant transformation. An ocean has many waves that change continuously. They are sometimes tsunamis, hurricanes, monsoons, tidal waves, or harmless currents that carry plentiful foods for various areas that its rivers go through.

Going through a transformation can be terrifying because you have adapted to one way of doing things. It works and so you've become attached to it. You are not certain of the things that will come your way after transformation. You don't know how people are going to react. But, to be very honest, none of that matters. The transformation stage is one where only you can make the decision to enter. It is a stage that you must brave alone. There will be no need (or room) for outside voices. Enjoy this stage. Transformation is your road to enlightenment.

Sweetness of doing nothing

Dolce far niente translates into "sweet doing nothing." **Dolce far niente**. What a beautiful, sexy phrase. We often tend to reflect and find understanding in our journey once we've found the sweetness in doing nothing. You know those moments I'm talking about. When it's just you and you only. That moment you realize that you are not lonely but alone with your true self. That moment when no one can judge your thoughts or action. That sweetness of just being YOU in the stillness of the present.

In the movie Eat Pray Love, Liz Gilbert (played by Julia Roberts) discussed the *dolce far niente* while visiting Rome. The part that I always look forward to watching is when Liz is in her apartment and starts reflecting on the experiences she's had with her ex-boyfriend David. She reflects on how broken and low she was in her life during their time together. She just sat there in her room (alone, not lonely) and reflected on that entire experience. She decided to write David a letter to express, not what she felt back then, but where she was now in her life. In the letter, she states the following: *"We all want things to stay the same, David. Settle for living in misery because we're afraid of change, of things crumbling to ruins… Both of us deserve better than staying together because we're afraid we'll be destroyed if we don't."*

We find our sweetness in our moments of doing nothing. We find wisdom in our reflections of past experiences. We find solitude in our quiet understanding. We begin to create opportunities to grow and become more than who we are presently. Like Liz, we can find strength in our transformation, if we allow ourselves to. We can accept and welcome constant change with love. We can find the beauty in *dolce far niente*. And if we find this to be true, we can also recognize that the immaculate experiences that brought ruin into our lives are truly beautiful gifts too.

Look Harder Into Your Vision

When we envision our future, the normal reaction is to get very excited. Your emotions run wild. We might have the urge to tell loved ones and friends what we see for ourselves and all the things we hope to experience in the future. But one thing that I've learned is that many people don't look at the full scope of their vision. They don't look hard enough. They simply glance at it, see the positive energy and smiles they will create at the completion of their goal. With that said, consider this: the people you are connected to today, are they connected to your vision for tomorrow?

Most of us never ask this simple yet hard question of ourselves. It's as if we don't want to deal with the reality that who we are connected to today could become strangers tomorrow. Not everyone will have the privilege to walk with you on your entire journey. There are many seasons in your life and they come with many changes whether it be relationships, friends, family members or business partners. Our visions are usually best in telling us what we need to accomplish or sacrifice. We just have to truly observe and adhere to the messages of our visions.

One of the hardest things a person has to do is let go of present relationships, even if they know it is hindering them from accomplishing their goal. The longer it takes to let go, the more detrimental their current situation will become. When you look at your visions, you have to ask yourself why your favorite cousin, boyfriend, girlfriend, relative, or best friends aren't in your vision. What are they doing today that cuts them out of your vision for tomorrow? This is an imperative question to ask yourself. I remember Oprah saying to a young lady in her audience, "Who do you want to be in the world? Not what you want to do. Not what you want to achieve. Who do you want to be in the world?" I've found this is clearly answered in your vision. Some of the people you are attached to now may be the reason your vision is blurry. Maybe your inner fears are causing you to not examine the details of the vision you have created for yourself. But please remember there is absolutely no room to be fearful when pursuing greatness.

Oprah went on to tell the young woman that sometimes you have to divorce your friends, as well as some of your family members. But if you handle them with love, they will come back if they are meant to be in your life. This might be true but until you look at all the details in your vision, you will never know who you need to serve those divorce papers to.

The Higher You Climb the Ladder

The higher you climb your ladder of success towards your personal greatness, the smaller your original circle will become. You will have to come to terms with leaving a lot of people and things behind. You will have to come to terms with this because the selfish wants and insecurities of others will become too heavy of a burden to bear while trying to move forward. You only have one life to live and you don't get a do-over. Dealing with and living through your success can be harder to do than with your failures. There are constant life decisions that you will have to make in order to be free and open to the idea of prosperity. When the majority of the people around you don't have a healthy work ethic or could care less about tapping into their higher power, you will have to be the rebel of the bunch. And rebels never have it easy. Never ever.

The Beauty of the Journey

The beauty of unleashing your greatness on the world is that you are actually doing God's work. Yes, you are in partnership with the creator of this beautiful universe. As soon as you give your all on a journey to manifest your true potential, God will begin to lead you places that you could never dream of. That's what happens when you pursue the vision you so long yearn for. These visions that we all seek to create, guides us to something bigger than we could ever imagine. The universe already knows what we want and what routes we will decide to take. But every so often, the universe will have us take an alternate route to inspire us to see bigger things and to expand our vision. At first, it's normal to question it with frustration but we must understand that it's only for a greater benefit.

The Effect of Desiring to Be Someone Else

When we desire to be someone other than ourselves, we are indirectly telling ourselves that we don't like who we are. People tend to worship people they believe are greater than them in some way. It's one thing to admire someone for who they are or what they've accomplished, but worshipping them is definitely off-limits. When people give up on themselves, their dreams, and ambition, they begin to live through other people's experiences. No one deserves our worship except God. There is no one walking this Earth who should be worshipped. Don't act like the light that you see in someone else isn't also within you. We are all vessels carrying a beam of light. Some people are able to tap in completely while others may have some difficulty. That doesn't mean that their light shines any brighter than yours. You just haven't learned yet how to turn your light on full blast.

Time is Honest

Time is truthful and will always be honest. When we waste most of our lives on things that don't pertain to becoming the best we can be, eventually time will tell on you. Time will let everyone you know at some point in time that you either wasted time foolishly or invested your time wisely.

To be great, you must respect and manage time as the greats. Not one second should be wasted. Do you know how many hours, minutes, and seconds are in a day? Get a calculator. Do you know how many days, weeks, weekends, and seasons you have in a year? If there are 4 weekends in a month, what will you create and experience during that time? Plan accordingly. This is how diligent you must be with each day that you have the privilege of living.

When you have an Olympian work ethic, you will be burning the midnight oil on many nights. There may be times where you won't sleep because the vision you have is so amazing that not one second should be wasted on sleep. Sounds extreme, right? It *is* extreme!. That's how you have to be with your time and vision. Time is of the essence. You must develop your sense of urgency. Tomorrow is not promised. All you have is today. You have to get up before the alarm clock. You have to be the first one in the office and the last one to turn off the lights and close shop. You have to want it so bad that going to sleep makes you feel guilty. You have to want it so bad that taking a vacation will be taking a bathroom break or a simple shower in the morning. Time is honest and you should be as well.

If you treat time with respect and appreciation, it will reciprocate your actions and show your greatness to the world.

The Cost of Greatness

The cost of greatness is expensive. Greatness is like high-quality designer clothes. It never waivers in price. You won't find it on sale. It wasn't intended for everyone, only the people who can afford it. Greatness is expensive. Everyone will have the opportunity to get it, but the work that has to be done is greater than achieving mere mediocrity. You have to be willing to give up a lot of your time whether it's leisure or with family and friends. The amount of sacrifice and late nights is the price of greatness. Massive amounts of people do minor things and expect a major league reputation. They expect the recognition of being called great when they are still in the minor league. The cost of greatness may be high but if you are willing to pay the price, you can be a member of this exclusive club.

Inventory Check Yourself

Where you begin in the morning and where you end up at night is very important to your growth and your impact on the world. Doing an inventory check is a vital part of your daily routine. A personal inventory check is one way to measure your progress both internally and externally. It is a personal reality check so you understand what you are getting from all the energy you are putting out.

For optimal results, do it once in the morning and once in the evening. It is very important to dissect the details of your daily routine. Also, it's important to recognize what you gained or lost within a day. In the morning, take a moment to check bank accounts, who your friends are, where you actually live, what state of mind you are in, and review all your goals (short term and long term). In the evening, before you go to bed, check the same areas that you did in the morning. See if you've lost or gained anything. This will help determine your daily success and failure rate in life. It will let you know what you need to work on and what your strongest areas are. Remember: inventory check yourself daily. Once in the morning and once in the evening.

Peace

As I am writing this, it is well after midnight. A eucalyptus spearmint candle is burning. The Forever Cool album by Dean Martin is playing in the background. *"No more doubts or fears/I've found my way…"* This is my peace and my peace alone. Peace is always available to you. All you have to do is detach yourself from the "noise"--the people, situations, and gadgets that create/promote chaos in your world. Staying attached to things that cause you to speak negativity over your life isn't winning. Some say it's very hard to cultivate peace around you when you're so used to keeping chaos around you. Hmmm… I'd like to think that when you are sick and tired of being "sick and tired", you will be more proactive to release yourself from those lifeless situations. I believe it would be just as easy as lighting a stress relief candle at midnight, turning off your television/phone, playing some calming music. And just being peaceful. Doesn't seem so difficult now, does it?

Be the Peace within Chaos

There will always be chaos somewhere. And if that somewhere happens to be where you are, you must look inside yourself to become the peace within it. We all have the power in ourselves to create peace. Even in the midst of chaos. There could be a riot going on right outside your door yet, in your home, there is peace. There could be tension in your home or at your job, but when people come around you, they sense your peaceful spirit. Peace is always available. All you need to do is tap into it and be it. It only takes one peaceful person to gather a collective group of people to bring peace to the country in chaos. We've all had moments where we've either created peace in a chaotic situation or ran to someone who gave us peace when it was needed. Not everyone wants to live in a hostile or chaotic environment. These individuals yearn and naturally gravitate towards people who have a peaceful spirit. They want to learn from them and become just as calm and peaceful. Be an example of peace. Never hesitate to help those who are attracted to your peace. They want to learn to be the reflection of what you are.

The Blessing of Leaping

Have you ever taken a leap? I'm talking about taking a leap into the unknown. Taking leaps that scare the hell out of you. Leaps so BIG that you'd have to yell at yourself, "What am I thinking? This is CRAZY!!!" Yeah, I'm a grand master when it comes to taking those kinds of leaps. Today, every day, is about just that- taking leaps and finding beauty in the unknown. If you don't mind, I'd like to share a personal experience that I've always cherished since the moment it first happened...

I had never flown on an airplane until the age of 22. About 6-8 months prior to me knowing that I would be taking this flight, I woke up one day mad and frustrated because I realized I wasn't truly living. To be very honest, school was boring to me, I was tired of seeing the same people. Doing and talking about the same thing day after day, year after year. Most people I knew didn't have the same passion as I did. I was tired of watching music videos of people popping bottles and "making it rain" (this is when an individual is in a night club and throws money in the air to prove that money is not a problem for them. The lies! The lies!). I was tired of watching MTV Cribs (More lies!). I was tired of being in environments where people never wanted to develop their aim to hit a distant target. I was totally done with that lifestyle. I wanted to go to Hollywood, California. I wanted to be amongst the dreamers and go-getters. I wanted to learn EVERYTHING from that type of crowd. I wanted to be in the running for greatness.

Then IT happened. An old friend of mine was reading a book called, "The Dream Giver" by Bruce Wilkinson. He told me that this book would change my life (I love when people tell me that because I'm always game for a positive change. Two days later, he finished the book and it was in my hands. Let me explain something to you. After reading this book, my life went into full transformation mode. It lit a fire under me. I wasted no time and called a cousin that lives in LA. I flew out there, and at age 22 my eyes were wide open. I ate sushi for the first time. I met and hung out with the VP of ASCAP (The American Society of Composers, Authors, and Publishers). I was invited to and attended birthday and dinner parties of some of the most influential people in Hollywood at that time. (I wish I could tell you about all the public figures that I inspired while there and the wisdom they shared with me, but you would have to come to one of my seminars to get that!) Before I returned back to the East coast, my cousin gave me a key and said, "Rah, from this point on, you are no longer local. You are now bicoastal. This is the key to the residence. I want you to remember that you are something special and you must think bigger, dream bigger, and make the world your playground."

When you take the leap, it's always going to be into the unknown. No one can truly know the outcome of the choices they make. You can assume but unless you have a crystal ball that can show you the future, you can never be 100% sure. That is why I say it's a leap into the unknown. Millions of people never take one leap because of fear. I like leaping into deep waters because there are all types of opportunities in it. It is untouched territory. Dolphin-like opportunities. Whale-like opportunities. Some not so great opportunities; I call those shark-like opportunities. But what good is s/he who never takes the leap? Their life ends up shallow. And we all know that no one is allowed to dive into shallow water. So I offer an open invitation to the great swimmers of the waters! Come out here with us! Take a leap! Take a dive! The more swimming partners I have – the BETTER!!!

Victories in Business

Being victorious in business comes in all forms. I've had my own fair portion of victories that I always love to share with my clients, fellow entrepreneurs or individuals I mentor. Many of my clients get a kick out of how I explain victories and the psychology behind it all. You see, when I am able to put together the right team to accomplish a big goal – that's a victory for me. When I am able to close a deal for the intended amount of money I pitched – that's a victory for me. When the meeting went smoothly and everyone understood the information and vision – that's a victory for me. With victories, come celebrations! There were times when I popped open bottles of Dom Pérignon just because everyone showed up to a meeting on time. That was a GREAT victory in my eyes.

Even though these are great victories to me, one must understand that there is a "Keep Your Feet on Solid Ground" mentality that must be kept. A company becomes DYNAMIC when it focuses on the big and small details that make that company run smoothly. Focus on the client. Focus on the product. Focus on the staff/team development. Focus on aiming to have every person with the company make it to work 15 minutes prior to the time they've been asked to come in. When the janitor at your office is inspired to come to work due to the company culture... When you've finally destroyed a bad habit that was hindering you from getting to the next level... To me, that's what being victorious is all about.

The companies that thrive for years are the ones that vessel people with an "underdog spirit" and leaders whose mindsets are focused. Here is something to keep in mind: underdogs are braver and more fearless than champions. (How else do people turn into champions?). Champions have nothing to prove when they reach their pinnacle of success.. Maxwell Maltz, M.D, F.I.C.S. once said, "When a championship team begins to think of itself as "the champions," they no longer have something to fight for, but a [status] to defend. The champions are defending something, trying to prove something. The underdogs are fighting to do something and often it brings an upset." Great business (wo)men have the mindset to fight for their clients, their team and their ideas. They come into the industry as underdogs with the intention of causing an upset to those who may have too big of an ego to see the changes that are happening in their very own industry. You know them, those "old ways of thinking" type people. When individuals and teams dwell on their degrees and awards, they set themselves up to be a Goliath. And we all know what happens to all the Goliaths that stand off against the Davids of the world. They fall.

As you tap into your greatness, you can create a lifestyle that will allow you to shine brighter in the world. Imagine you're a boxer. When you step into the ring (your path), you aren't defending the championship belt – you're fighting for it. Every time we, as creators within this world, create something new (product/service/etc) we are actually stepping into the ring. We are laying our championship belt on the line to see if we deserve whatever reward comes from it each time around. Remember: stepping into the ring at all is a victory in itself.

Chicken and the Hawk

There was a chicken. This chicken lived in a chicken coop. In this chicken coop were 99 other chickens. Each and every day this chicken would do everything with the 99 chickens. He would eat with the chickens. He would sleep alongside the other chickens. He would play with the other chickens. He would work with the other chickens. Whatever the other chickens did, this one particular chicken did too.

The chicken never questioned his existence nor did he believe anything was wrong with how he was being raised. Until one day he noticed something very strange…

One specific morning, this chicken woke up in the chicken coop feeling quite strange. He went about his normal routine: greeted his family, greeted his friends, and headed over to where breakfast was being served. "Something is definitely different," he said to himself. On that particular day, he had questions that he wanted to be answered. He went to his friends and asked, "I noticed that when we eat, everyone is full but I am still hungry. Why is this so?" His friends replied, "Don't worry about that. You are a chicken and we all eat the same portions." He then asked, "My voice seems louder than everyone else. Why is this so?" They replied, "When that happens, lower your tone. You are a chicken. You have to keep your voice with the same tone as the rest of the chickens."

He nodded in agreement but still he felt something was wrong. They started playing and he realized that he was now bigger than the rest of the chickens in the coop. He asked, "Why am I bigger than the rest of you? I notice that when we run I am running faster than everyone else. I notice my body is lifting off the ground. Why is this so?" The other chickens replied, "If you see this happening, just slow down and run at our pace. You shouldn't allow your body to lift off the ground. It may seem that you are bigger in size, but that is okay. You just have to remember that you are a chicken."

The young chicken nodded in agreement and then looked up at the blue skies. He was amazed by the colors of the sky, the fullness of the clouds, and the brightness of the sun. He had a new feeling and vision. He started to inquire about what could be outside of the chicken coop. He knew what the answer would be if he asked his chicken friends and family, but he asked anyway. He trusted their words and advice. They took care of him and they were everything to him. They were the same. He walked up to one of his cousin chickens and asked, "Why are we in this coop? What is outside of this chicken coop, cousin? His cousin replied angrily, "NOTHING! STOP ASKING THESE POINTLESS QUESTIONS! YOU ARE A CHICKEN! YOU BELONG HERE WITH US! NO MATTER WHAT YOU THINK, OR HOW DIFFERENT YOU THINK YOU ARE, YOU ARE STILL A CHICKEN! YOU WILL ALWAYS BE A CHICKEN!"

He was very hurt by the tone of his cousin. So he walked away into the open area in the chicken coop. Just then, five birds flew across the coop. When all the chickens saw the birds, he watched as they all ran into hiding. One of the birds that was flying over the coop noticed the one chicken standing by himself, flew down and sat on the fence.

"Why are you down here in this coop?" asked the bird. "I live here. This is my home," said the chicken. The bird was very confused by his answer. "You live down here? In this chicken coop? With these chickens?" said the bird. "Yes, yes I do," said the chicken.

The bird realized what could have happened to this chicken in his younger years and began to ask him the following questions, "Look at me. Don't you look like me?" The chicken took a long stare and then looked at himself and replied, "Why, yes. I do look like you." Then the bird asked, "Don't your feathers look like mine? Doesn't your voice seem louder than the other chickens in the coop? How about when you play, don't you run faster than everyone else?" said the bird. "Oh my, I surely do!", said the chicken. It was a notion that the chicken could not comprehend. He thought, *What is going on here? What is happening??*

The bird replied, "Since no one has told you yet, I will be the one to tell you. You are not a chicken. You are a hawk!" The chicken could not believe what he was hearing. How could this be? All these years, everyone was telling him he was a chicken. Everyone he was around had always told him to slow down, eat less, be more gentle, stay on the ground. But that particular day, at that very moment, a bird that made every chicken run away in fear, flew down to tell him he was a hawk and not a chicken.

The hawk offered the chicken (which had now found himself to be a hawk) the opportunity to teach him how to fly. And after just a few tries, the once chicken took flight out of the coop and became who he had always been. A hawk!

Same Sky Different Direction

It is paramount to remember that even though birds are created to fly, not all will do so. The hawks in the sky may surround you, but that doesn't mean they are necessarily going in your direction. In the sky, there are no boundaries or borders. From the ground's perspective, what you assume is flying may actually be falling. You have to elevate (your thoughts) and begin to take flight to recognize their true direction.

Not all hawks soar. There are so many reasons for a hawk to spiral down. Many hawks spiral downward because they didn't hunt much or because they are waiting to feed off of other hawks. Some hawks don't take the time to allow their wings to develop. Not allowing their wings to completely develop makes it hard for a hawk to fly long distance. When the seasons change and all birds have to fly to a different region, certain birds won't make it. It is vital that you make yourself aware of these downward-spiraling hawks. They will try to latch onto your wings and bring you down with them.

Don't Turn On What Will Throw You Off

If you want to be successful, don't turn on what will throw you off. Don't turn on the television if it will throw you off your studies or planning. Don't turn on the phone's ringer if the people who will be calling you are breeding toxic conversations that will throw you off your focus. Success comes in many forms. And so do distractions. Make sure you can recognize them both when they are around you. Be aware of your surroundings so you will be able to differentiate between the two.

Authentic Light

Authentic is defined as a means of undisputed origin; genuine. It comes from the Greek origin word "authentikos" which translates to principal or real. The word light is defined as the natural agent that stimulates sight and makes things visible. It is also known as the understanding of a problem or mystery; as in, enlightenment. As human beings, we are all designed to beam out authentic light constantly. There are so many people who don't believe their light is of value so they dim it or turn it completely off. Society can make us feel that being our true selves (light) in the world is a totally bad thing. Society can cause us to downgrade our genius and brilliance. And for what? To give someone else the opportunity to enhance their own ego by using another person's light? No, no, no, I don't believe in that and neither should you.

When you are of authentic light, you:

- embrace your real character.
- are honest with yourself and the world.
- give respect and show love to others unconditionally.
- live with purpose.
- have an appreciation for life.
- are thankful and show gratitude.
- live by your word and say what you mean.
- do not dim your light in the face of adversity.

False Light

The word false is defined as not in accordance with truth or fact; incorrect. It is appearing to be the thing denoted; deliberately made or meant to deceive. As a person who wants to achieve and unleash their greatness on the world, why would you want that type of light? Why would you want to be far away from what is real? No man or woman attains the goodness that is meant for them. When anything is meant for you, it will come naturally. Some will attain many things when they project a false image of light in the world. In reality, the benefits do not belong to them. They are only entitled to the repercussions of being fake and being a person who exudes false light.

When you are the vessel of false light, you:

- are not your real authentic character.
- act phony for selfish reasons.
- find ways to use other people's light for personal glory.
- show no genuine appreciation for life.
- are one way in public and entirely opposite in private.
- don't keep your word.
- invest in the growth of your ego, rather than suppress it.

Authentic Light vs. False Light

Authentic Light is what you want to give all the time. When you give off authentic light, you have control of it. All that comes to you will be for you. You want to stay away from the false light because it's not real. All that comes to you isn't truly for you. This can range from honors to relationships you attracted from your false light. When you are authentic, things move smoothly, in grace and with love. It is appreciated and well taken care of. Let me give you an example.

Authentic Light	False Light
You receive blessings that you've earned.	**You are stealing blessings**
	(When you falsify your light, all that comes to you isn't authentic. It is all an illusion as the light you are illuminating to the world.)
Thankfulness Intensifies	**Stress begins to arise**
	(This is due to looking for new ways to sustain the false light that you are illuminating while trying to enjoy the blessings you've received.)
Expansion of your territory	
• Greater yearning to know thy self • Higher level of thinking • Deeper gratitude for relationships	 **You will begin to breakdown emotionally and mentally.**
Deeper focus and openness to the universe	**All blessings will become a burden**
• Light illuminates • Energy intensifies	• The feeling of loss of self will be magnified • Chaos stage will be completed

Power

Power should not be defined by how much control you have over others, but how much control you have over yourself. This is important if you want to preserve your light. You can only control the vessel in which your light is occupying. It is a waste of godly time trying to achieve control over someone you never created. You can be an influence over others, but to have complete control over them is an illusion.

Throughout history, there are stories of individuals who tried to control a mass group of people. That came at the expense of losing lives, legacy, hurt, and pain. One may assume they have complete control but "assume" is the key term here. And you know what happens when you assume, right?

Abused Power

Many men have tried to use their power for selfish reasons and eventually failed terribly in the long run of things. Hitler was a prime example of this. There was no greater good in how he mistreated the Jews. Historical events such as the Holocaust and slavery are eternal stains on our global past. With great power comes great responsibility no matter where you are from. We all have some type of power and when developed daily, can make a significant effect on the world. Why not use that power for the greater good? Think about it. There are no praises given or songs written about those who abused humanity or polluted the world with their selfish acts of greed.

Developing your power for good or in order to make a more positive impact on the world is **awesome**. All power that helps and affects multiple people around the world is exceeding power. That is the kind of power that I would say has God all in it. Your power inspires people to help communities have clean water. Your power inspires people to stimulate the economy. Your power helps people find purpose in their lives. Transcending power is a universal energy that billions of people can feel when unleashed. It is one of the more gentle forces in the world that people love to experience.

Learn to control your emotions in certain situations. Learn to develop great habits that will enhance your influence in the world. When you focus on controlling your actions, you begin to illuminate and cast more light into the world. When you are continually investing in yourself, your return will be constant individual freedom. Don't try to control others. Focus on controlling you.

Seeing Happiness Cultivates Joy

Happiness is one of the words we use to describe joy. Happiness isn't the actual feeling of joy. It is the confirmation that you are experiencing joy. Joy is a pure emotion in which gives you the positive vibes that confirm you are surrounded by happiness.

Happiness is your favorite color. It is the sports you love to participate in. Happiness is your favorite holiday. It is your best friend. Happiness is your favorite song and movie. Happiness is the memory you are constantly telling everyone you meet. It's the male/female you have a crush on. Happiness is the person you call your soul mate. It's your favorite book, favorite number and place you like to visit. This is happiness. All these things I've listed cultivate the emotion called "JOY."

It's a beautiful situation when you look at happiness and joy in this way. Joy must be in your life continuously. You only have one beautiful life to experience. We tend to attract different things into our lives and each thing we bring into our lives cultivates a certain emotion. It's in our best interest to bring in things that will intensify our emotion of joy.

Always Maintain Your Joy:

1. Maintain your sense of stillness.
2. Have aspirations that breed daily aspirations.
3. Visualize these aspirations and feel them every single day.
4. Show your joy in random acts of kindness.

Happiness & Joy is contagious

- When you have happy friends, your joy increases.
- If your friend has a happy friend that you don't know, your happiness increases.
- You affect people you don't know indirectly.

Light Language

Be Light with Your Words

Language: the tool we must understand and use to create a life and the peace we want

Do you understand the power of words? Words can shape a life. Words can build empires. Words can destroy legacies. Words can shift a culture. Words can describe a moment. Words can create a moment. There is power in our words. There is light in our words.

There is a cyclical relationship between word and thought. The words we speak out of mouths start off as a thought in our heads. We know they are there because we listen to the voices of our inner self. Once we release those thoughts, they become words. Words that combine and form a sentence. Words that create a sentence and form new thoughts in out head. When we control our words, we control where they go and what energy they hold. Like us, words, are vessels of light. The lights within those words are fragments of our own light. The words we speak are an extension of us.

Our words hold great power so we all must be very cautious with them. Where we place them. Who we choose to be recipients of our words. Recognizing the energy we are actually putting into these words. A definition or meaning of a word is the spirit of that word. Our words have life. Once they are released from our mouths, they leave behind our legacy.

We live not by our words alone but also by their meaning.

We must always be conscious about the words we birth into the world because our words have the power to create life or bring death. Our words can create more good or create more bad in the world. Words can cultivate peace or create horrible wars. When we take control over our lives, we have a better grip on our words of life. When we use words to speak death into another's life, we have to understand that this is a representation of ourselves. When we decide to be lights within the world, we make a conscious decision for all of our creations to be full of light. This is definitely inclusive to the words we speak.

Life and death are in the power of the tongue. The great Dr. Maya Angelou stated, "Words are things, I'm convinced. You must be careful about the words you use or the words you allow to be used in your house. In the Old Testament, we are told in Genesis that in the beginning was the word, and word was God and word was with God. Words are things. You must be careful… Someday we will be able to measure the power of words. I think they are things. They get on the walls. They get on your wallpaper. They get in your rugs, your upholsteries, in your clothes. And then finally into you." This is true. When you walk into someone's home or environment, there are words that you use to describe it. These words have already been in the room and things placed in it. All you did was acknowledge what words were in the air and space. I hope this didn't fly over your head and seem too deep. I mean it to be taken quite literally.

Have you ever seen someone wear a shirt with just one word branded across the front? That person meant to give the world their message. They wanted to make a statement, to make you understand the energy that is connected to that word. That is why it's imperative to notice the clothes you wear.

Inventory check: What do your shirts, pants, and shoes say about you in words? Do they assist people that are around you to create positive light words in your life? Or do they give off the words of negative energy and dim light?

We all wear invisible words that hold some type of life within them. Our invisible words are in our eyes, our facial expressions, our smile, our posture, the way we walk, the way we stand. Each word has a spirit and history attached to it. Words, invisible or not, are on everything in the world. They are on books, business buildings, cars, clothing, phones, bodies, household appliances and anything that the human eye can lay its eyes on.

Inventory check: What words are on you? What words have you accepted to be attached to your life? What words have you detached yourself from? What words will you stay away from, from now on? What words will you attract on your life? The more words of light and positive energy you have on you, the better.

Transferring Energy Light through Words

We all have conversations with people for various reasons. We have conversations with individuals to give direction, share theories, ideas, emotions, experiences, and our viewpoint of the world. When connecting to another person, be aware that it isn't just you that is speaking. It's you and all those who've impacted you prior to that moment. The people who raised you, taught you, studied with you, hurt you, loved you, advised you, worked with you, created friendships with you, entertained you, and even inspired you in life. Each person has implanted something in your spirit that has sustained. Connecting to these people have molded your thoughts which in turn you used to create a view about life. From these individuals, you've adopted some of their words and developed them in ways that fits you. These **words** come together and form a **sentence** that will either continue to **imprison** you or **release** you from the internal prison you may have been in.

Be Careful with Your Attention

When you give your attention to negative people, gossip and bad news, you give it the wrong power. You are nurturing a negative energy and playing a great leading role in making it grow. This is not what one does when trying to illuminate the positive light that is within. Stay away from the gossip or kindly ask to have that conversation continued at another time without your presence. What good comes out of talking about the flaws or mistakes of another beautiful soul if no one in the circle wants to help that person? What good comes from watching bad news all the time? Change the channel, turn off the television, or subscribe to a different magazine. We all know there are areas and people in the world who focus on harming the world but it is not your place to dwell. Focus on being the answer to a problem or a producer of more good in the world.

Your attention holds great power. When you are a reflection of love and light, many people and groups will want your attention. You must choose wisely who and what will get your attention. Be careful because all attention isn't good attention. Nothing is more harmful than giving your power of attention to someone who is harming another person who truly deserve your attention.

The Consequence of Hesitation

> "Men often hesitate to a beginning because they feel that the objective cannot be achieved in its entirety. This attitude of mind is precisely our greatest obstacle to progress. An obstacle that each man, if he only will it, clear away."
>
> - Gandhi

Hesitation is a sign of fear. It is a sign that one is not confident in the action that they must do. All gut feelings are signs pointing you in the right direction, no matter what outside voices may say. When we hesitate on our goals, we hesitate on our dreams. The longer we take to pursue our goals, the longer we could possibly be blocking our or someone else's blessings. We could be the answer to the prayer that someone prayed last night. But until we embark on the path to achieving our goals and dreams, only then will the person who prayed for us, will be able to see us (the answer to their prayer).

We all hold a light for someone in the dark. We all carry unlimited blessings which is why it is possible to be a blessing every single day of our lives. Even when we pass away, we can still be a blessing by the things we've done and accomplished while on this earth. But when we are living, we must be fully engaged in all that we do. We must not hesitate with the one life we were blessed with. You hold a cure that someone's child needs. But if you are hesitant to go to school to learn how to be the great doctor you are destined to be, how can this child receive their blessing? Someone needs a friend and you are hesitating to make a call. You need not hesitate because you are the answer to so many prayers. Be not hesitant. Be not of fear. Be of confidence. Be of light.

Fall in Love Everyday

Falling in love is a habit that I never want to give up. I learned about falling in love daily from one of my very good friends in New York City. One day she and I had the most amazing outing in the city. We went for tea, walked through the park, had a great conversation about life, and talked about what we've experienced prior to becoming friends.

After hanging out with friends and family, I have a tendency to send an email or text message letting them know how I truly appreciate the bonding moments. It was no different with her. She followed up with an email reflecting the same energy in her words. But what really grabbed me was her statement about how she fell in love with me for that moment. She stated that every day she falls in love and on the day that we were together, I was the person she fell in love with. Not only did I appreciate her words but I felt the same way.

Ever since then, I have always made sure I am aware of what I fell in love with that day. It could be a person, a moment, an email from someone, a picture, a trip.... Falling in love daily allows you to be totally attentive to the things that bring that feeling of joy out of you. Love constantly travels and you need to be aware of where you can find it daily.

There are moments when I think of a person and just love them wherever I am. We might not have spoken in awhile, but I still love them whole-heartedly. I may meet someone for the first time and after a great conversation with them, I let them know that I love them at that very moment with all my heart. This is the norm for someone with light. Not just any light, but transcending, unprejudiced love. Agape love.

When you love, love unconditionally. Love from the bottom to the top. Here are some things I do in order to perpetuate love. Hopefully one or more of these tips will help you learn how to fall in love daily.

- Think of individuals who you've had in-depth and beautiful experiences with. Send them a thank you message as a reminder of why they are loved or tell them why the experience you all shared made you appreciate living even more.
- Reflect on places that bring out the best in you. Ask yourself why do these places bring out the best in you. Try to go there as often as possible.
- Randomly send a short and awesome message to people who bring warmth to you every time you connect with them.
- Create a love moment with someone. This can be with a friend or family member or someone you always wanted to connect with. Just something of a small gesture that will make them and you smile.
- Do something for yourself, by yourself. Just indulge in the moment. Acknowledge the emotions, the joy and appreciate it.
- Fall in love daily and you will become an example of love. You will exude love and will attract even more love.

Beauty is Perfection

Beauty is perfection. *"There's a lot of beauty in ordinary things."* Beauty has no real boundary because each person sees beauty in various people, places and things and in various ways. Beauty was created with such perfection that it is mishandled all the time. Beauty is to be admired because it is at the highest form of creation. Each person was created with beauty. Not just a few chosen people, everyone is created in their highest form of beauty. I always say, "We were all created perfectly imperfect to fulfill our purpose perfectly in a world where people tend to focus on the imperfections."

Think of a flower after it has completely blossomed. We admire it because it is at the highest level of its beauty. It is alive and full of energy. But what happens to the flower when it is admired by perfectly imperfect people? They pick it from the ground because they want it for themselves. They may pick the flower out the ground just to see if the scent matches the beauty. They may want to use it to decorate their home. They may want to use the flower to give to another. And use the beauty of the flower as a symbol of how much they love or admire another individual's beauty. But is this right?

Beauty can only be preserved when it is connected to the source. A flower is no longer connected to its source when it is picked from the soil. It automatically begins to die as soon as its stem is broken or roots are uplifted from the ground. This goes for individuals as well. Why should we use the beauty of another person or thing to signify our admiration for another person's beauty? Use your own beauty as the only point of reference. No two things are the same or possess the same beauty and that is what makes it perfect.. Your beauty is in the time you share, your facial features when you love something, your hugs and kisses, your heartfelt conversation. All of these things are a part of your beauty. If you ignore using them in the highest form, you are cutting your own stem. Your thoughts on paper, your gaze, your laughter, your talent are all part of the perfect you. Don't be afraid of your own perfection.

Beauty should be admired in its perfection. Why pick the flower? Just look at it while it's connected to its source. Understand that it's most beautiful and perfect when it remains untouched. Its beauty will be able to survive through its allotted life span if it is not tampered with. Understand it is playing its role in the universe and as long as it is in its own beauty, all is perfect.

The Beauty in Silence

Every day I try my best to master the art of silence and quietness. I believe it is a daily ritual that we all must practice. I remember attending a 3-day peace conference and listening to some of the world's most amazing teachers of peace and spiritual enlightenment. Some of my teachers for that conference included His Holiness the Dalai Lama, Deepak Chopra, and Dr. Terri Kennedy, who taught the Gandhi Effect. During one of the courses I attended, a spiritual teacher stated, "Silence is the pure voice of the universe." This means that you hear ALL within all that surrounds you. Silence is said to be golden and this is the absolute truth. When we are in silence and quietness, we can hear the truth we seek. We are preserved in the silence of the universe. We find grace in silence and quietness. We can see things clearly in silence and quietness.

I specifically remember one summer when I recognized that I'd gained profound insight while I was in the stillness of silence and quietness. It happened while spending some time with my grandparents on their porch. It was such a beautiful day outside and something told me it would be great to visit the "young" couple who has been together since they were high school sweethearts. As always, when I arrived, I received the biggest and warmest smile from my grandmother. Followed by the big kiss that I have been getting from her since the day I came into this beautiful world. After receiving and giving love to my grandmother, I transferred that same energy to my grandfather. His southern grin and deep shout of my name are the confirmations that I was also appreciated and loved by him. We gave each other a cool man pound of the hand and followed up with the usual "What's going on witcha?" It is always the same and for me, it is always beautiful.

That day, my grandparents sat together on the family bench that faces the street and I faced them by sitting on the long porch sills. We talked, laughed, and reminisced about everything. But something happened that day that I will never forget. When we finished talking and laughing, we all just sat there in harmony. We sat there in the stillness. We sat there in the moment. We sat there in silence and quietness. My grandfather gazed into the openness of the skies and my grandmother watched the birds fly back and forth. There was something so beautiful about it. No outside noise except what God created. No phone ringing. No cars passing by. No music playing. Just three of God's beautifully-made vessels being filled with the moment.

As I watched them, I thought about the experiences these beautiful people went through when they were my age. The friends they made and the friends they lost. The relatives they loved and lost. I wondered what they had experienced that they'd never told me. It was something I could only ponder while being in silence with them. I immediately felt this burst of love from them and all they were doing was being still in the moment of silence.

I was happy for them because of who they had become. I was sad for them for all they'd lost. I was proud of them for all they'd accomplished. I was praying for their continued sustenance. I was in complete joy for them. In that moment of silence I asked myself if I would be able to be like this at their age. I mean, here are two people, in their late 70's and 80's, who have been through all that they could with the one life they were given. And here they still stood in love and in light.

The question hit me hard because at that very moment, I realized that, in years to come, I would be them. All that I care about and find so important now will eventually be forgotten. All goals and aspirations will be in the wind. I realized that there is no need to be attached to things of "today" because, in 40 years, they won't be there. The only thing I knew for sure is that, in that exact moment, love was present. Grace was present. Joy was present. All together in silence. Since that day, I have been able to see clearer than the days before I sat on that porch with my grandparents. Since that day, I have had a better understanding that you learn more in the silence and/or in the company of love. "Silence is the pure voice of the universe."

Each day when you wake up, sit in silence. No need to speak or make noise. Just move in silence. Don't let noise be the distraction to what the universe is trying to say to you. Action in silence is more effective than moving with the noise of the parade. Make it a daily ritual to spend at least 15-30 minutes in silence in a healthy environment. See what comes to mind. Acknowledge your thoughts and then let them roam where they may. Silence and quietness have no boundaries or limits. It's the voice of the universe. There is no end to the space we are in. Silence. Allow it to be golden in your life.

Silence the Noise

You must quiet all noise if your goal is to share your light in the world and unleash your greatness. You must be aware of artificial noise and the voice of the universe when you are in the stages of development. You must be able to distinguish the difference between the two.

Artificial noise is all the things that distract you from developing, finding out and knowing who you are. This type of noise is the technology you are currently using: social media, music, the empty conversations, the dead relationships that you are holding onto, the empty conversations you are having, and the energy that fear brings forth. Artificial noise will decay our mind and body, leave our light dim and our spirit lost. It does not feed us the substance we truly need within the universe. Only the universe in its most authentic voice can develop us and show us the true way.

This brings us to the voice of the universe. "Silence is the pure voice of the universe." When we are in complete quietness, the silence of the universe can be quite loud. The universe will speak to your spirit and guide you to where you need to be. The majority of people are led in the wrong direction because they are drowning in artificial noises. We can only hear the universe's voice when all noise around us has been completely turned off. The universe speaks only truth which may feel like a sharp stab at times. This is because we are not accustomed to what the truth sounds like. We have grown attached to the lies that artificial noises tell us.

When we sit in quietness and listen to silence daily, we will eventually began to pull back the layers of our false self. We begin to listen to the source that created us in our purest form to help us get back to becoming whole again. Silence is the voice we need to listen to in order to grow. Many lights become dim or die out because they made a decision to follow the wrong direction from the artificial noise they've been listening to.

Be a Lighthouse for Sailors around the World

A lighthouse is a tower structure designed to emit light from a system of lamps and lenses and use navigational aids from sailors at season inland waterways. Lighthouses mark dangerous coastlines, hazardous shoals, reefs, safe entries to harbor, and can also assist in aerial navigation.

You are a lighthouse to all sailors and pilots around the world. It is your responsibility to stand tall and strong throughout all seasons to guide sailors away from harm. It is your responsibility to make sure you show these sailors how to find their way back from the sea. It is your responsibility to continually develop yourself so that your light doesn't burnout or become dim. There is a need for more lighthouses in the world for people who are making the decision to sail out into the world. They are all trying to see what life has to offer them, but they will need guidance. They are going to need someone to light their path if their light isn't completely developed as of yet.

It is important that you take this very seriously because there are many sailors who are lost at sea. They could be lost due to constantly making the wrong decisions in life. They may not have a strong crew to help them manage their boat through the storms they encounter at sea. Whatever it may be, you are responsible for illuminating your light as far and as bright as possible. When you walk your path in appreciation for your purpose, you will be able to assist others in finding a way back to the source. We are all creators connected to The Creator of the magnificent universe. Never ever forget this. Live by light, my friends.

D3=F Philosophy

Discipline x Dedication x Determination = Forever

When I was 18 years old, and attending my first year of college, I was exposed to many teachings that I wasn't able to access while living in my city of birth. I was walking through the campus on my way to the library to study for a class I can barely remember. While en route, I thought about the equation E=mc2, created by Albert Einstein. It intrigued me that this man, who developed the general theory of relativity, one of the two pillars of modern physics (alongside quantum mechanics), created the mass–energy equivalence formula $E = mc^2$ (which has been established as "the world's most famous equation"). I thought to myself, what if I created an equation that could grant success to any human being on this planet? Whether they were considered a failure or genius in school, it wouldn't matter. This equation would be a pillar to extraordinary greatness and legacy.

So as I headed into the library, I sat my young, ambitious self down and began brainstorming. I don't know the exact moment it came to me, but I do remember what I felt when it did. D3=F. It was like a cloud being cleared and the sun shining alongside a rainbow in the middle of the day! From that point on, I would begin teaching the method of D3=F. The equation became my own personal philosophy and method to personal achievement. I knew that I had to be the example of its authenticity or it would be considered just a hoax.

Over the years, I have used this equation to reevaluate and reconstruct my own personal work ethic as well as on my relatives, friends, and clients. I use this to determine what the outcome could be or would have been had I stuck to the three quantities. Let's take a look.

THE EQUATION TO GREATNESS

DISCIPLINE

Discipline by definition, and verified by my research, is a systematic instruction intended to train a person (sometimes literally called a disciple) in a craft, trade or other activity, or to follow a particular code of conduct or order. Often, the phrase "to discipline" can carry a negative connotation. This is because enforcement of an order–that is, ensuring instructions are carried out–is often regulated through punishment.

Discipline is a course of actions leading to a certain goal or ideal. A disciplined person is one that has established a goal and is willing to achieve that goal at the expense of his or her individuality.

Discipline is the assertion of willpower over desires and is usually understood to be synonymous with self-control. Self-discipline is to some extent a substitute for motivation, as in when one uses reason to determine the best course of action that opposes one's desires. Virtuous behavior is when one's motivations are aligned with one's reasoned aims: to do what one knows is best and to do it gladly. Continent behavior, on the other hand, is when one does what one knows is best, but must do it by opposing one's motivations. Moving from continent to virtuous behavior requires training and some self-discipline.

This quality is essential in mastering your craft or methods to tapping into your greatness. As you progress, you meet many different individuals. You will attract many different opportunities. You will have an oasis of options that can take your eye away from your overall goal or purpose. Having discipline allows you to remain steadfast on your daily rituals, practice, and training. Discipline gives you the extra strength to say no when (you think) you truly want to say yes. It trains your focus and intensifies your determination daily. Discipline is an art that all great individuals master. Discipline will shine a bright light on your path. It allows you to rebuild, reinvent, restructure, reshape, and reflect on the old you. Discipline is an action that tests your mind, body and spirit to prepare you to embark on the next level with a gladiator state of mind.

DEDICATION

Dedication is defined as a feeling of very strong support for, or loyalty to, someone or something. It is the quality or state of being dedicated to a person (yourself included), group, or cause.

Dedication is a quality that is essential to the loyalty and value of your vision and self-worth. This quality is needed to activate faith. Dedication signifies that your vision is priceless. That no matter the cause or situation, you will not falter. It is the quality leaders have when they are with their followers. It is the quality of the student who is writing their thesis for college. It is the quality of the individual who stands up day after day for the fight to bring equality around the world. Dedication is that unwavering faith that you will succeed. It is the sibling of discipline. Dedication tests your will and limits on how far you will go to achieve your goal (e.g. unleashing your greatness).

DETERMINATION

Determination by definition is firmness of purpose; resoluteness. It is also the process of establishing something accurately, typically by calculation or research.

Determination is a quality that is essential while tapping into your greatness. As you progress on your path, you will most certainly get hit with various obstacles and it will seem as if all is against you. You may experience sickness, death of a loved one, death of a friendship, bad business opportunities, sleeplessness, monetary problems, and anything of the like. But having determination will allow you to fight through the hurt and pain. You will go through the agony of temporary defeat because you are aware that while you may lose battles, you can still win the war. Determination is like the blinders you see on horses when they are racing. Nothing can distract them from the left or the right. The only thing that matters is crossing that finish line. One must have unwavering determination if they want to unleash their greatness on the world.

EQUAL FOREVER

While doing my research, I found that the **equals sign** or **equality sign** (=) is a mathematical symbol used to indicate equality. It was invented in 1557 by Robert Recorde. The equals sign is placed between two quantities that have the same value, as in the equation. In mathematics, the equals sign can be used as a simple statement of fact in a specific case, or to create definitions, conditional statements or to express a universal equivalence.

I believe that when you are in possession of all three qualities (discipline, dedication, and determination) your name and all that you've done will last forever. I believe your name will echo in the hallways of eternity. You will leave a legacy for generations to come. Your family will be able to have something to boast about; something that will make them proud to share your last name. I think about the people we still study today who lived so long ago, but because they embodied the D3=F equation, their name will forever be on our lips, in our books, in our history. These people include Gandhi, Martin L. King, Mother Theresa, Nelson Mandela, and so many others from around the world.

PERSONAL PHILOSOPHY

As you begin to tap into your own personal greatness, you will begin to transcend into a philosopher. I have studied so many of the greats, past and present, and they have all been great philosophers to those seeking to be on their level. Each person had their own belief system, quotes they lived by, and even a list of core values and standards for themselves.

When I was discussing the D3=F Method, I was definitely thinking of one of my great mentors, Bruce Lee. He is a supreme being as far as ranking philosophers and greats over the years. Bruce's daughter said, "What made him amazing was that he brought his thoughts, beliefs, and philosophies into physical being." The philosophical principles he lived by were heartfelt. There is one philosophical quote of Bruce's that I apply to my life daily: "Using no way as way, having no limitation as limitation." He created a symbol that would become the visual symbol of this quote. Bruce put this symbol on everything from business cards to a gold medallion that he wore wherever he went. This was his constant reminder of D3=F.

YOUR PERSONAL PHILOSOPHY & METHODS

By using all the tools mentioned in this book, you will eventually tap into and unleash the greatness within yourself. But first you have to do the intense work to find your own voice and words. What will be your words? What will be your methods and philosophy? My D3=F philosophy is a critically necessary equation in my life. It is my way of life. There is nothing I cannot do. This statement is based upon the established thoughts, methods, and philosophy I have set for myself. What statement of life are you going to set for yourself?

MIND IS EVERYTHING

The mind is supreme. The mind is where all things, both powerful and weak, are stored. What you believe, experience, taste, touch, smell, and articulate is all in the mind. It's something to think about when you are having meaningless conversations and embarking on activities that belittle the greatness within you.

Let's discuss belief system for the moment. I need you to understand and be fully aware of how this works because I want you to be able to unleash a great deal of light into the world. A belief system is considered a set of mutually supportive beliefs. The beliefs of any such system can be classified as religious, philosophical, ideological, or a combination of these. These beliefs are a strong reason you are where you are today. These beliefs also give reason to why you fear whatever it is you fear and why you make certain choices.

Your mind must be in total shape before embracing what will come with unleashing your greatness. Kai Greene, world renown bodybuilder, stated, "Mind is everything. If you believe you can't do something then you can't. It's like you have to save your own life. No one is going to save it for you." What you believe will determine the path in which you will truly walk. If you want to be the example of pure greatness and walk down the path of greatness, you are going to have to have a great belief system. Anything less than that is unacceptable.

We all have the capability to be great, but not everyone possesses the belief system necessary to tap into and unleash their greatness. All that you have learned from when you were a child up to the present needs to be reviewed and questioned. You have to pick out and see which beliefs that were passed down to you. Those are the proverbial balls and chains holding you down. Your parents could love you for eternity, but that doesn't mean they didn't raise you to develop weak belief systems.

All the greats had amazing and intense belief systems. Let's take Michael Jordan as an example first. Michael changed the game of basketball and had such a powerful effect that millions of people were saying, "I wanna be, I wanna be like Mike!" Yes, when you have a strong belief system embedded in you, this can happen at any level of your life. MJ was completely focused when he trained for games. Once he went to the gym to train, as soon as he walked through those doors, nothing else mattered. The main and only thing in his mind was going strong in the weight room.

When it came to basketball, MJ's mindset was the true key to his greatness. He could tell you that it was more than dribbling and shooting the ball in the basket. John Robert Thompson, Jr., former basketball coach for the Georgetown Hoyas, said, "If you can put your mind to whatever it is you want to do, good things can happen. So before anything else happened with MJ outside of that game, that shot gave him the idea that he could be greater than what people think and surpassed any expectation that he may have had for himself."

MJ once said in an interview, "My greatest moment in sports was when I made the game-winning shot against Georgetown. I believed that if I had any doubts about playing in the big leagues with the big guys, that shot gave me the confidence to believe that I belonged where I was." You see, it was MJ's belief that he belonged exactly where he was. Even if he had missed the shot, he still would have been where he belonged. But the question is, would he still have believed? The answer is yes. MJ believed he had the potential to do and be anything he put his mind to. This is the kind of belief system we must have. Knowing that nothing is impossible. Nothing is too far from our grasp. We can have anything and everything we want as long as we are willing to put the work in.

ASK MYSELF ABOUT MYSELF

I always tend to get deep with those I teach and consult because that is where the seeds of greatness are. They are deeply implanted in our soil. When you want to find the source of anything, you have to dig deep to find it. I can recall discussing with myself (because sometimes you have to talk to yourself) about my belief system. I do this from time to time because I strive for greatness. And you must do an inventory check on yourself daily.

The conversation went like this:

Me: Do you believe in God?
Me: Yes, Rahfeal Gordon, I believe in God.
Me: Do you reflect God?
Me: Yes, I do. Not only do I reflect God, I believe he dwells within this beautiful and handsome man that is ME!
Me: If God dwells within you, as you, doesn't that make you a creator and a person of love?

I paused for a moment and really thought about the question. I am a creator. I am love. I am of goodness. I am the creator of my universe and all that I allow to dwell within it. I can choose if I want to roam in hell or heaven in the time I am given. This is amazing. This is scary. This is overwhelming. This is powerful!

Our belief system can alter our entire universe. It takes constant development of the mind in order for it to manifest all that we are trying to achieve and become. It is the most powerful tool you have on the planet. It is also the most underestimated and underused tool that I've seen, thus far, in my life. People tend to not use it properly and allow anyone to corrupt it with toxic and detrimental core beliefs.

You must develop beliefs that will push you to the highest mountain you can climb in this lifetime. You can't worry about what other people believe. You can't control other people. You can only control yourself. You can, however, influence other people with how you live by your beliefs and by proving what the effect on life has been because of them. Developing the mind is never an easy thing. Breaking down old beliefs and setting new ones to follow is always easier said than done. Have you ever recognized a belief system that you had in your mind for over 20 years and then realized that it is wrong? Now you have to get rid of it and create a whole new system. That's no easy task. It's going to be a tough process but well worth the fight.

Michael Jordan said that the mental part is hard because you have to take all that you have learned over the years and apply it to all that you do. This is the absolute truth. Adding to what MJ said, if some of the lessons you learned along the way aren't in accordance with your new belief system, you have to first deal with its impact on your life and then you can make the correction. You can only hope that what you learned all these years in your life weren't in vain and hold you back from unleashing your greatness most of your life.

You Need Reminders

It is important to have reminders when you are doing the work. You need reminders because you don't want to get lost in the moments of success and lose sight of the purpose of your pursuit. We all have heard about people in various industries who have lost themselves in the fame and fortune, ruining their hard work. It is a path to destruction when you don't place reminders in your life.

We need reminders to stay focused in order to achieve our personal greatness. Reminders could be having your friends keep you in line when you get too close to the edge. It could be a letter that you read when you're feeling lost. It could be a picture or some type of note from someone that admired what you are doing. Reminders like these are a necessity. I have a notebook filled with various pictures that are constant reminders. I have a pile of letters from 6th and 7th graders whose school I visited. They wrote about how motivated and inspired they were during and after my speech. Things like that help to remind why I am on this journey.

Results of Having No Reminder

- Ego gets big. You begin to think it's all about you.
- Lose site of the mission and purpose.
- Most of your actions will be in vain.
- At some point, you will go through an inner storm that could either transform you or leave you in ruins.

Results of Having Reminder

- You will stay grounded.
- Ego will be in check daily.

- Nothing you do will be in vain.
- All that you do can be measured.
- Sense of respect and admiration you receive when you are reminded why you do what you do.

Stability and Instability

Stability by definition is the quality or state of something that is not easily changed or likely to change. It is the quality or state of something that is not easily moved and someone who is emotionally or mentally healthy. Stability is an ongoing process. No one is ever stable for his or her entire life. Find me a man that has been stable since birth and I will introduce you to a person who has been walking since the first moment they came out of their mother's womb. When you are in constant development of self, you will begin to yearn for balance. And balance is a reflection of stability.

We can find the birth of stability in our minds. When we create peace in our minds, we are creating balance within our universe (our lives). Peace has and will always begin in the mind. Balance has and will always begin in the mind. Stability will forever occur in the center of our mind. The reason why many people don't experience stability is because they simply focus on the instability of things.

Instability by definition is the state of being likely to change. It is the tendency to change your behavior very quickly or to react to things in an extremely emotional manner. Many people focus on the instability of circumstances around them, which in turn makes them attached to that current situation. Focusing on the imbalanced areas around you is the main culprit of why you are having issues and problems. Many individuals become burdened down by the imbalance of things they focus on.

It is a priority to create stability in your life because all that you are connected to will be affected by its current state. Whether you are balanced or not, your family and friends will taste a piece of it. You are reading this book to help you gain the necessary tools to reach your highest self in all areas of your life. What good is it to read a book to help you develop your light and achieve your personal greatness, yet you are constantly focusing on the instability of things? Everything begins in the mind and you have a responsibility to cultivate peace within it so that you can keep your life as stable as possible.

Personal Mission Statement

Having a personal mission statement is a great way to stay tuned in to what you are supposed to do daily. I learned about creating a mission statement from a leadership coach a few years ago while attending his seminar. It made sense to me since I was in the stage of my life where I wanted things to be simple and clear (this was one of the visions I had for my life). The following information is for you to develop your very own personal mission statement. It will be your guide to all that you do.

A mission statement is a two to three-sentence statement that describes what you want to accomplish within your lifetime. Whatever it may be, it cannot be accomplished next week or even next year. It is a lifelong mission that you will be aiming to accomplish every day of your entire life. Your statement is clear, simple and accurate. It tells all those who come into contact with you, who you are, why you exist, your reason for being. It will constantly challenge and develop you until your last day here on this earth.

My personal mission statement is only 1 sentence but is very effective for my own lifetime goals.

RahGor Mission Statement: To be one of the greatest global speakers and entrepreneurs from America while showing individuals all over the world how to make their dreams and goals a reality.

I will give you an example on how to construct yours using one sentence. The first part of your sentence should pertain to what you want to achieve for yourself. The second part should be what you will accomplish or do for the others in the world. Here is an example; John's personal mission statement is "To be the greatest pianist in the world while using my talent to develop new ways to use music as therapy in the medical field." Another could be "To be one of the top surgeons in my state while finding a cure for cancer." Do you get it now? There is a balance in these personal mission statements.

When it comes to your personal mission statement, you must memorize it back and front. It has to be embedded in your subconscious mind. Every day that you wake up, you must state it. Throughout the day, you must check to see if all your actions are focusing on the mission. When you are getting ready for bed, you must reflect on your activities of the day to see if it helped you get closer to your mission. You must state your mission loud and clear before bed to yourself so that even while your body sleeps, your mind is still working on ways to make your vision a reality. This is *your* mission. You have to take it personal.

Personal Mission & Opportunities

The great thing about having a mission statement is that it now gives you a complete focus in life. You can use it as your guide, compass, and a reminder of why you are making certain choices and grabbing hold of some of the new opportunities that come your way. While I am on the topic of opportunities, let me stress something crucial to you. Every opportunity that comes your way is not always a good opportunity.

Your personal mission statement helps you weed out all the opportunities that are not for you. Listen. You have to understand that bonding with friends every Friday night was okay THEN. But now that you actually have a mission created, going out every Friday night will kill your progress. Yes, having VIP tickets to that concert sounded great THEN. But now it's actually self-damaging if you have an opportunity to present in the early morning for potential business investors. Having a focus is great because it will work out your "discipline muscle." You will begin to question everything you do to make sure you are staying on the path you've chosen. This will help you make better decisions and take stronger steps towards your vision.

Transcending to Become Something beyond Thoughts

Transcending has always been my primary focus once I found purpose with my life. All great global leaders that have touched this planet have transcended beyond the customary thoughts of man. Look back in time: from Aristotle to Einstein, from Jesus to Martin Luther King Jr., from Nelson Mandela to Steve Jobs. Each of them tapped into something so deep within them, and so far beyond the norm, that no matter the color of your skin, religious background, family structure, origin of birth, their words were embedded in your mind. The effect of their impact is incomparable.

I previously gave you the three stages to transformation (chaos, ruin, transformation). What comes next is transcending. This stage has an effect not only you, but on the entire universe.

How to Transcend

There is no one certain way to reach the stage of transcending. When you reach the level of transcending, your greatness touches all. I call it the "God Level." The reason I say this is because GOD has no color, race, ethnicity, origin of birth, opinion, or limit to His greatness. In the level of transcending, your true greatness affects all in ways that no one could fully imagine.

Achieving this level is the result of constant and continuous personal development. You have grown accustomed to continually working on your mind, body and spirit. You have fully committed to working on not confining your true self to the labels that people try to put on you. You have gotten rid of labels and titles. You no longer allow it to feed your ego. Now you have to look beyond the boxes that society attempts to put your in. Now you can recognize that each label you accept is a responsibility and burden that you are allowing to be placed on your life.

In the transcending stage, you must constantly think on a global level in order to develop and create various energy (action) in this beauty of the world. You have to leave behind the local mindset and shift into a global mindset. You have to learn to move in the spirit when you've decided to do something. You have to be aware that whatever you involve yourself in, also involves your spirit. And if you don't feel it in your spirit, it definitely should not be your priority.

Many people have experienced a transcending moment at some point in their lives. Most of them will tell you that it cannot be explained. That it can only be described by going through the experience itself. Everything is in sync with the universe when this happens. The vision is clear. The words are clear. The actions and thoughts are clear. It is a moment attached to nothing but affects all things. It is when a music artist makes the best album. It is when a painter creates a masterpiece. It is when an athlete breaks records. It is when a writer composes the most astonishing literary piece that millions of people can understand and relate to ("The Alchemist" for example). Transcending is powerful and if you are looking to live in the light as a light, you must be willing to sacrifice all things comforting and all things conforming. Only then will you be able to reach a level where you can touch someone no matter who they are or where they come from.

Be Attached to Nothing

Being attached to nothing is a great path to take when transcending to your higher self. When you become attached to "things", those things automatically attach themselves to you. The weight of these things hold you back from growing and developing. Not being attached to anything allows you to keep your mind clear and calm. And a calm mind is a necessity while on our journey. Scientific research states that a calm mind is the source of a good and healthy life. I would believe so because what does a chaotic mind bring? A chaotic life. And as people of greatness, we aren't about that life.

Having a calm mind, you are fully able to be observant of yourself and all that is around you. You must know your truth to make a real decision and to take real action. You will never be able to look at anything objectively if you do not first look at the situation with reality. Decisions based off a false reality is a time-consuming dead-end. There is no true path in trying to fill a false reality with a false purpose.

As you gain experience and learn ways to become greater than what you imagine, hold on to the fact that real happiness and real peace will never come to those in competition with/ within the family and community. There is a sense of joy and humbleness that comes with experience. You must be truthful, honest and courageous for your mind to be peaceful and compassionate. If we want to transcend and have peace within our family and community, it has to begin with us. Then it will trickle down to our children and household.

Mastery of Change

We all must be masters of change. Change is forever. Growth and development, that is change. When we acknowledge our blessing in seeing another day, that is change. When we realize that our lives are heading towards our moment of transcending, this too is that awesome action called change. When we have removed distractions or disturbances, we can begin to move higher in life and to cultivate the inner peace that one must have to be a master or teacher. I remember when His Holiness the Dalai Lama said to us during the peace conference, "You must have true inner peace and master your studies before you can teach others. Change the self then you will be able to change the environment. Prayer and meditation won't change you or society. It is an action with applied knowledge from studies." We cannot be the voice of change, transformation, or enlightenment if we have not tapped into these sources within ourselves. We must have a reflective life of all the things that make transcending possible.

The universe is within us always. The emotions of what we yearn are always within us. The wealth we seek is always and will forever be within us. The best way to find what we seek is to be a representation of it in the world. It is only then that all that surrounds us become the reflection of the universe that is within us.

The Effect of Transcending Yourself

When we find our inner peace, when we find our true light, when we begin to transcend our lives, our presence illuminates wherever we are. People will begin to ask you questions so they can figure out how they too can become the light you display. When you have cultivated your own sense of PRESENCE, you won't need to strain for attention because you will always have it. You will not need to impress or force yourself onto others. You will be a completely radiant star that attracts other radiant stars.

There is a process to building a house. There is a process to building a school. There is a process to having a healthy life. All these things take time but through a process they will become what they were intended to be. Our process of transcending our light will be different from many, as no two paths can be identical. But the methods we use during the process are always the same.

Process of Elimination

We should always inventory check ourselves while going through our process. We have to be like a child in our development stage. Children learn more by observing rather than taking months to develop a plan, agenda, or system. They are more fearless yet less structured when developing. They see things for what they are and they ask questions (But how? But why?) until even the person they look to for answers, can't come up with one. In that very moment, they begin to make decisions based on their own observations. Observation is key.

There is no need to justify yourself.

You must continually review what your good qualities are and what has held you back from being a positive light in the world. Once you have "observed" your list, you can begin the elimination process. Trying to suppress negative qualities rather than eliminating them is where most go wrong. When you suppress, you are only storing unnecessary weight in your life. You allow things to linger. You are stuffing your inner closet with old clothes that you can't wear anymore. You become a hoarder. All the light that is supposed to fill your life cannot shine because your "stuff" is blocking its path. You must eliminate what hinders your process. Old habits, old views, old opinions no longer have a place in your world. Period. Joy and sadness cannot occupy in the same place. You would be crying and laughing at the same time, which, to me, is a definite indication of internal conflict. We all experience making bad decisions with good intentions in mind. But bad decisions are usually made when clarity is absent from us. We forgot something. We didn't let go of something. We weren't as ready as we thought. Always observe and know when and what to eliminate if you want to elevate.

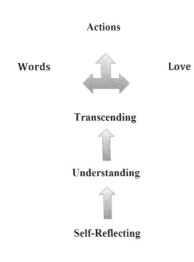

After the Transformation Stage, we begin to self-reflect and observe what we did to become our new selves. As a result of constant reflection, we begin to understand why it was necessary. After understanding, we can begin to do bigger and greater things in the world without limitations. All people and situations can be positively affected by all we do because we've done our homework. We've gone through our process and can be an example to others who are just beginning their own process. With this comes a sense of power and a new responsibility.

CREATING QUANTUM LEAPS IN YOUR LIFE

A quantum leap is **defined as** an abrupt transition of an electron, atom, or molecule from one quantum state to another, with the absorption or emission of a quantum. In simpler terms, it is a huge, often sudden, increase or change in something. We tend to have quantum leaps in our lives at moments when things seem calm or normal. You may get a phone call, email, or text that can cause the calmness of your life to turn into the rollercoaster of a lifetime.

When quantum leaps occur, they are not necessarily due to big or life-altering circumstances. They can happen due to the smallest change in what we have connected to as our norm. Something as small as receiving a one-word text message can create a quantum leap in your life. You can make your entire life experience to this point a quantum leap that would impact your new life for years to come. Does the idea of that scare or excite you? Are you going to make a change? Then, read on!

How to create a quantum leap in your life

First, observe where you are, acknowledge how you got there, and understand why you are there. We are the sum of all things we have experienced, learned, and created in the world. We are where we are because of what we accepted, believed, lacked, gained, and what we felt attached to because in some way we felt it reflected who we are.

We have to take a good, hard look at the sum of these things. Then change something. Change your phone number. Find a new way to get to work. This will begin the process of a quantum leap. The sum of our decisions about all the little things is what allows for a major explosion in our lives because they differ from what you've made a part of your everyday life. Although they are small details, seemingly, go for the drastic and monumental change. It will have a significant impact on you.

For example, you could stop eating meat. Just by eliminating meat from your diet will definitely begin a significant change in your body, health and mindset. It won't show at first but over time, the leap will be tremendous. About 2 years ago, I canceled my phone service for 6 months. Six. Whole. Months. It was the most stressful and the most liberating experience I have ever felt in my life. The first 2-4 weeks were so stressful and different that I didn't know how to react to this new availability of time. I knew I had become an addict to my phone. After all, my business, personal, and social life were dictated by what came through the phone. After the first few weeks, the initial shock wore off and I realized I was quite content without it. By the 3rd month, I felt like Superman. It was absolutely amazing to watch the transformation. Everything in my personal and business life skyrocketed. It came out of nowhere. This was a quantum leap moment for me. To this day, I am still affected by the decision to get rid of something as insignificant as a cell phone.

Understand the fact that the sum of your small changes will create a drastic change and then you will be prepared for your BIG LEAP. Sometimes we fail to realize that something we do every day is warming up for a leap in your life. Something as small as going to bed at 9:00pm rather than 11:00pm, may be the reason you are not accomplishing a particular goal. Simply making a change in bedtime could be exactly what you need to have the best energy for the day. How about reading the newspaper every morning rather than listening to the morning radio? How about blending a green drink for breakfast instead of pancakes or a bagel? Any one small change made to your everyday ritual will cause a major shift. You will experience a quantum leap.

Quantum Leaps Can Be Disastrous

Leaps on a major scale can be just as dangerous as it is good for you in your life. When I think about this, I automatically think of the BP oil spill that began on April 20, 2010 and ended September 19, 2010. This disastrous oil leak was documented as lasting for 87 days. The US government estimated the total discharge of crude oil was 210 million US gallons. It claimed the lives of eleven people and hundreds, if not thousands, of wildlife animals in the Gulf of Mexico. It is considered the largest accidental marine oil spill in the history of the petroleum industry. BP estimated the company's total spill-related expenses were close to $37.2 billion.

This event was definitely not expected by BP but what do you think was the reason behind it? Not paying attention to the little details. Time and time again, the newspaper and the news channels would read BP's statement: "*Many* human and technical failings in a risk-taking corporation that operated in an industry with ineffective regulatory *oversight*." BP blamed the accident on "mechanical failures, human judgments, engineering design, operational implementation and team interfaces." BP's partner, Transocean, said, "In both its design and construction, BP made a series of cost-saving decisions that increased the risk, and in some cases severely." It was more than just one change but essentially they were small decisions continuously that made the event a quantum leap for disaster.

When you have reviewed and analyzed where you want to make a quantum leap in your life, make sure it is a positive one. No need to be shy or bashful with the action. Go for it! Make sure you are doing all the right things for your experience. Whether you are changing the types of books you read or the color of your home. Make the change while knowing you are preparing yourself for a quantum leap to occur.

RahGor K-Studies to Help You Reach Your Greatness

In this final section of the book, you will find a few well know individuals who I took the time of studying over the course of a few months. Each individual, I believe, holds various keys to help you unlock your greatness along the journey. You will learn about their work ethics, belief systems, growth process, and the key elements that they all share that made them great in their own right. You will find out that they are all similar in one area but totally different in another. But that is what makes them iconic and walking monuments of excellence. I hope each individual K-Study inspires you and uncovers all the possibilities that are in front of you.

Yo-Yo Ma *world-renowned cellist*

At the beginning of my early 20's, I had the opportunity to assist Yo-Yo Ma before his concert at New Jersey Performing Arts Center. For those who don't know, Yo-Yo Ma is an Award-Winning Cellist from the United States. He has 75 albums and has received 15 Grammy Awards. On the day of his concert, I observed his managers and how the production team prepared the stage for the concert. I have always loved being backstage. This is where the magic happens. It's where you see how the artists prepare to inspire, entertain, and captivate the people that came to see them perform. That day, there wasn't much that had to be done for his concert except putting out a few chairs and stands for musicians to place their notes and making sure sound and lighting were excellent.

While backstage, I overheard someone say, "Yo-Yo Ma is preparing to go on stage to rehearse. No one is allowed in the theater at all. Musical genius is about to practice." Throughout the day, people were saying how important and magnificent Yo-Yo Ma is as an artist. I thought to myself that this was my opportunity to see him in action. All by myself. So I quietly walked through the production hall, up the backstage stairs, into the theater balcony hall, and slowly open the balcony door. I gracefully and quietly walked in unnoticed and just watched. I sat there and fell into the moment. There was no one in the theater but me, him, and God. The music was so transcending, so breathtaking. It felt like he was playing for angels that were dancing in the aisles. I was there for about 30 minutes. Just watching. Just feeling. Just illuminating. Just appreciating. Just embracing the harmony of life.

I think about that day often and use it as a reference point of how doing what you love will always inspires others. Yo-Yo Ma and I never met directly, but we both shared in the same experience. He created it and I was blessed to be a witness to his creation. Have you ever witnessed something that made you feel happy just be alive? Have you ever watched someone in their purpose and it put you in a trance for that moment in time? If your answer is no, then you haven't been paying attention to the small details. (Refer back to the section "How to create a quantum leap in your life." Whether you are a teacher or an artist, a scientist or janitor, an entrepreneur or cashier at Starbucks, a lawyer or stylist-when you are passionate about what you do, you will always be an inspiration to others. You will have people taking precious time out of their schedule just to experience your energy. They will go out their way just to admire you. Being a source of inspiration is a blessing that should never be taken for granted. People like Yo-Yo Ma are important in the world because they are examples of what happens when you truly develop your God-given talent.

I always aim to give that same experience during my seminars. There are times when I walk on stage and people are already cheering. I haven't even spoken yet, but the energy in the room is already transcending. Most times, all I can do is bow my head and give thanks. Knowing you have the energy to inspire others with your talent is a gift within itself. Don't waste it; we all need it to live.

Jim Carrey *world-renowned actor*

Jim Carrey, the award-winning actor, is simply an awesome spirit. As a kid, and even now, Jim always seemed so cool to me. When I get the opportunity to meet him, I know his personality will confirm this. (Wait. Did I just put that into the universe? You know what that means… A picture of Jim Carrey and RahGor will be coming soon!) I want to use my buddy, Jim Carrey, for this particular RahGor lesson. There was an interview that he did on February 17, 1997 on the Oprah Winfrey Show that has been labeled one of the best Oprah interviews. Here is the breakdown.

Around the year of 1987, Jim was considered a broke actor (as most budding actors are). He wasn't making any money in his career (yet) and was hustling hard to make his dream come true in Hollywood. Jim's mentality was pure gold. During his broke days, he would visualize himself getting big movie roles. He would drive to a very well-known residential area in LA and visualize himself actually living there. He would visualize all the good things he wanted to come to him. In the interview, he stated that he even took it a step further by writing out a check for $10 million dollars for "Acting Service Rendered" and dated it November 1995. He gave himself 3 years to accomplish the goal. And right before Thanksgiving in 1995, he was offered $10 million dollars to play one of the two main characters in the movie "Dumb and Dumber".

Pretty cool, right? I would like to add that what many might overlook is that Jim had a very strong work ethic. Always remember that faith without works is dead. You can visualize things coming to you all you want, but if there isn't a quality work ethic behind it, you are ONLY dreaming. Then the time you spent dreaming will become a HUGE regret later in life. Let's not let that happen. Add visual training to your daily routine along with intense ACTIONS! See what you want, create a strategy, and then GO HARD IN ACTION! I need you to work hard EVERY single day until that dream and vision are something you are actually experiencing. Will it be easy? NO. Will there be sacrifices? YES. Will there be pain? OF COURSE. Will it happen overnight? DEFINITELY NOT. Will it be worth it? YES! YES! And YES!

High rewards come at a high price. The price can come in the form of sleepless nights, away from family/loved ones for a long period of time, no social life for a few months, giving up some of the things you love most, or moving to a new state or country. It may come at a price of facing your biggest fears head on.

The price can impact you dramatically, and if you begin to have doubts, ask yourself, "Is it worth it? Do I want it badly enough?" If your answer is yes, then ask yourself, "How far am I willing to go to get it?" These questions should be able to put things into the right perspective for you. Think about Jim and how far he has come over the years. He has traveled the world and inspired millions of people using his talent. He had talent, he had faith, and he had a healthy work ethic. Learn from the greats and make sure your work ethic is impeccable.

Bruce Lee *world-renowned martial artist and actor*

You have to be unorthodox with your work ethic to surpass all the levels necessary to attain your greatness. Bruce Lee ranked supreme in the world of martial arts due to his work ethic. Bruce collected over 2,500 books pertaining to all types of combat. It didn't matter from what origin of country, western, eastern and even modern styles he studied. He collected all types of books on philosophy, psychology, self-motivation and even fitness training. Bruce believed in studying every aspect of his craft in order to perfect his own. And that is exactly what he did.

There is the famous story of when Bruce had a back injury due to a fight. It was during his time of healing (stillness and quietness) that Bruce found his true purpose and calling in martial arts. Bruce spent time developing his theories and philosophies of martial arts. His work ethic became his way of life. He was a perfectionist and driven with constant intensity to master all that he could with his talent. 24 hours a day, 7 days a week, Bruce drowned himself in his craft daily. He would have private one-on-one session with students in his home and teach his little children all that he could about the craft.

Bruce believed that all types of knowledge is self-knowledge. He was a self-educated man. He believed wholeheartedly that people could express themselves through movements and soon enough, people began paying him to teach them the art of expressing the human body. Bruce work ethic transcended beyond the physical activities and tapped into his mental development. His core beliefs and value system transformed into something extraordinary.

Empty Your Mind

Bruce's belief was if you want to master your craft or want to become the great vision you have for yourself, you must be like water. He said, "Empty your mind, be formless, shapeless like water. If you put water into a cup; it becomes the cup. If you put water into a bottle, it becomes the bottle. Water can flow or it can crash. Be water, my friend." Being like water is a great concept to embrace with your work ethic because it means you can adapt to any condition given. You can be as gentle or as aggressive as you need to be when necessary. Just as water.

When you empty your mind, you allow yourself to be attached to nothing. You are mentally free from all the worries, doubts, and fears that could hinder you from rising up in your greatness. You want to be able to move in whatever way necessary and with great speed and accuracy while working on yourself. It's not an easy task but once you began to fully grasp the concept and embody the statement, you will truly begin to transcend.

Bruce had a student who was having a difficult time with his training. He constantly would be beaten by Bruce. As he lay on the ground, he said with a frustrated tone, "There's a lot to remember." Bruce, sat there, calm with a grin on his face and replied, "If you try to remember, you will lose. Empty your mind. Be fearless. Shapeless." Then went on to say, "You are not ready. Like everyone else, you want to learn to win but never accept the way to lose." What a lesson to learn while working intensely to reach a level. You must accept being defeated, whether it's of your own doing or by others. You must be willing to die to be liberated from loss or losing. All these things free you internally. As Bruce has said, "You must free your ambitious mind and learn the art of dying."

Express Yourself with No Limitations

Expressing yourself is difficult in a society that really doesn't give you the true freedom to do so. Bruce said that it is easy to put on a show and to be cocky. But to express yourself, your true self? That is very hard to do. "If I tell you I'm good, you'll say I'm boasting. But if I tell you no, you'll say I'm lying," said Bruce after being asked if he was superb in martial arts.

Your work ethic allows you to express yourself freely. Your work ethic comes as a lion's roar to the world that you are king of your jungle. It signifies that you will stop at nothing to defend what is yours. It is an opportunity to be either the lion standing on his rock in the savanna or the hyena being chased across the open fields.

Bruce Lee Work Ethic Philosophies

Here are some of Bruce's Philosophies to reflect on while mastering your craft:

- The individual is more important than any established style or system.
- You have to train to be one with your craft. Train to be one with self.
- Combine natural instinct with control. This will bring forth harmony.
- There are many ways to achieve your greatness. Use no way as the way.
- An idea is very much like a sculpture- not to add on, but to hack away the unessential so that the truth will be revealed, unobstructed.

Will Smith *world-renowned actor and music artist*

Will always says he has a great time with his life. He loves living and believes that living life is something we cannot fake. He also believes that greatness is within us all. His life's work is for the world to be a better place because he was in it. It's one of his philosophies that we should have to make every group we come into contact with, better. And for this to happen, we have to be at heart from the start.

Throughout my studies on Will, I quickly took note of how he also wanted his life, work, and family to be meaningful. "If you are not making someone else's life better, you are wasting your time." says Will. When it comes to the aspect of purpose, Will states, "It's like when you wake up in the morning and your life means something to someone other than you. Then you have a purpose. If you don't do the things you gonna do or dream of doing, that person's life will suffer." Will is very firm on his view that the purest form of joy is to live in service to humanity, family and so forth. I love the fact that he understands that we are all energy. "Energy is infectious. I can infect you positively or negatively. I can affect how you go home and deal with friends, family or significant others. That's something flawless. So if you affect someone /people positively, there is no way that you're not winning at what you do."

> *"It's what you love that you have to dedicate your life to."*

When you work, you must work super hard. Will stated, "The separation of talent and skill is one of the most greatly misunderstood concepts for people who are trying to excel. Talent, you have naturally. Skill is only developed by hours and hours of beating on your craft." He stated that he excelled by having a ridiculous, sickening work ethic. While a person may be sleeping, Will is up working. While one guy is eating, Will is working. Simply put, Will goes HARD! Are you able to handle this type of work ethic? Time and time again, people like Will have succeeded beyond the norm because they learned that no formula will succeed unless you are intense with your work.

Will Smith's Belief System

Will's system of beliefs is one to admire. He states that your talent will fail you if you don't perfect your skill, if you don't study, if you don't work hard or dedicate yourself to being a better person every single day. "I am not afraid to die on a treadmill. You may have more talent than me, smarter than me, but you will not beat me on the treadmill. You are either going to get off first or I am going to die." says Will. It's quite interesting that he puts his life on the line when it comes to his work ethic and vision. (Hmmm I believe you may have read that *somewhere* before.).

> "I want to represent an idea. I want to represent possibilities."

This statement signifies Will's level of consciousness is immaculate. He lets us know what his missing is and doesn't care if people respect it or not. "I believe I can create whatever it is I want to create. The first step before anyone else in the world believes it, is YOU have to believe it." Will says. I was watching one of his interviews, and he stated that great and successful people must have a disillusion quality about them. You have to believe something entirely different from the masses. Being realistic is the most traveled road to mediocrity. Why be realistic if you want to be great? Be *sur*realistic.

The Sickening Work Ethic

When it is time to work, Will is ready. He doesn't believe in a plan B because it will distract you from plan A. Will has said that people make situations more complex than they really are. "You must have an obsessive and desperate focus with all of your might, creativity, and heart." Attacking everything he feared has, allowed him to break free and have a superhero mentality.

Will didn't have any experience at the beginning of his acting career. So when he was cast for the Fresh Prince of Bel Air television show, Will put his drive into overload. He was so focused on winning that he memorized the entire script for the first six episodes. The entire script. His co-workers can recall seeing him on screen mouthing the lines of the other actors while they were speaking. Will was not going to let this opportunity pass him by. He had a relentless force and determination to prove to himself that he belonged right where he was.

> *"Just decide. As soon as you do, the universe will begin aligning the stars for you."*

Will has traveled the world and everywhere he goes, he constantly keeps his head held high. It is something his mother instilled in him while growing up. He states that he does this to confirm his belief that he is deserving of everything this planet has to offer. "If we dream something, if we picture something, and if we commit ourselves to it- that is a physical thrust towards realization that we send out into the universe." I couldn't agree more with you, Will. There's no point in being scared of your greatness when your reason for being here is to be great. It's the truth. Will says that you can't be scared of the truth because it's the only thing that will remain constant. You have to dedicate your life to your truth, the thing that you love wholeheartedly.

"If you get your priorities straight, it's really simple," says Will. Being great is as simple as making a decision. Make a plan and just do it. Just decide first because when the changes begin to occur, you won't stress because you already made the decision way before the choices were brought in front of you.

Finally, Will believes you are the five people you associate with. Look at the 5 individuals you are closest to. If you don't want to be those types of people, you know what you have to do, Will advises. We all have the opportunity to tap into our true selves and put something into the world that could change millions of people lives. Be aware of this and make a decision on how and when you will do it. Make a decision right now and let the universe guide you to the how.

Mike Tyson *world-renowned boxer*

Tyson was a great person to have studied during the process of writing this book. I learned quite a bit about the Mike Tyson THEN and the Mike Tyson NOW. Even though I tried my best to focus specifically on his work ethic, I realized that his daily life and his work ethic were one and the same. There are plenty of videos and documentaries of Iron Mike, which made the research entertaining, inspiring and intriguing.

Iron Mike Training Routines

Mike used to wake up at 4:00 am to run. After doing this faithfully for 8 years, his body began to automatically wake up without an alarm clock. He believed that his competitors weren't doing this so he would have a better advantage over them. Following his 4:00 am run, he would go back to bed for a quick nap and then be right back up by 10:00 am for breakfast. Monday through Saturday, sun up to sun down, Mike trained an estimated 55 hours a week and sparred 200 rounds. This is the work ethic that created a boxing icon.

Mike was trained by the BEST coaches in the boxing world. He absorbed everything his coaches told him while in training. All of Mike's past trainers, during an interview, stated that he was truly a perfectionist. He would receive insight or instruction on one day, and he would spend countless hours trying to master it. He would return the following day already knowing how to use the moves they taught him. They had always been in awe of Mike's work ethic and mindset.

Mike, along with his coaches, spent the evenings reviewing videos of his training and analyzing his workouts. There was never a moment wasted on things that weren't an asset to the development of his talent. Mike was an obsessive student when it came to boxing. He not only practiced in the gym, but at home as well. He not only studied boxing techniques, but he also studied boxing history. During his spare time, he would study the boxers who reigned before him and their methods. Mike always said that 85% of the fight is mental.

Mike stated that the most difficult part of boxing is the training. The easiest part was the actual fighting in the ring. When preparing for a boxing match, he and his entire team would fly to the location of the upcoming fight, no less than 5 weeks prior to the main event. That's not to say that he flew with an entourage, just his core team members. His team became a family. They lived, ate, worked out, and socialized together. They all moved in unison.

When he first came into boxing, he felt he could excel at it and in turn, gain recognition. So, he dedicated his entire life to it. Mike trained like other boxers at first, but then got to a level where he began adding a few innovative methods of his own to have a competitive edge over his opponent. His team created a method when training Mike with his combination punches. They would label each move by a number. He mastered these methods and combinations so well that whenever his coaches called out a number, he just threw the corresponding punch. Because he memorized the combos to the point that he didn't have to think about it, he just sprung into action. "Everybody thinks this is a tough man's sport. This is a thinking man's sport. A tough man is gonna get hurt real bad in this sport."

For those 5 weeks before the fight, all Mike did or thought about was training. He said it could get boring because the process is repetitious but he totally loves it just the same . Over the years, Mike transformed himself from the inside out. Similar to all great and iconic individuals, he became somewhat of a philosopher himself. Mike became more proud and confident about himself. And his growth was proven tremendously during his boxing career. The boxing world was changed because Mike changed himself. He tapped into his greatness and unleashed it into the world.

Iron Mike's Belief System

When I was watching a documentary of Mike in his prime, his energy and the way he spoke of his belief system excited me. "My favorite part of training is when the training is over and it's time to fight. I know I am in supreme shape and no one is going to beat me. And when the fight is over, I say wow. I am going to do this next time." His thoughts were transcending. He had no doubt in his mind that he would be the greatest boxer in his time. He said the first thing to do is think you're a champion. He developed his mind and body in the Catskills of New York. He was away from the streets, pain, distractions, and his coaches kept him busy all day with training. He was isolated and alone from everyone he knew for one reason. To be the greatest boxer of his time. Mike was afraid of no one.

"Every man must believe in himself. He must have the confidence no matter what the situation. You must face your problem. When you want to be the best in the world, there will always be disappointments. And you can't be emotionally tied to them cause they will break your spirit," said Mike. Doing the thing you hate as if you love it, that will take you higher. Constantly pushing yourself and testing your limits. He went on to say that when we have something in life we want to accomplish greatly, we have to give up our pleasures. To give up what comforts us (temporarily or not) for our goal, will cause us to forget our sensitivity to our fears. You will feel as though there is nothing to lose. Sacrifice is a necessity.

Iron Mike Results

It was hard to find boxers to spar with Mike because he was strong with both hands. The majority of boxers are dominant with only one. Mike was so dynamic in the ring that he was knocking out at least two guys every day of the week when in training. The coaches had to bring in professional boxers to spar with him because he was destroying his amateur sparring partners. Mike didn't care who stepped into the ring with him. He didn't care if you were considered the greatest boxer or not. The moment the match started, Mike already saw himself winning and so he fought fearlessly. If you had enough heart to get in the ring with him, there was no mercy for you. Mike would knock people out in the first round. Some thought he might just be lucky or that it was a fluke. It was unbelievable to watch, unimaginable even. But it sure did happen, over and over again. It made me see that with rigorous training and development of our minds and belief system, we can maneuver through any of our obstacles with ease.

"Sometimes people don't have the determination, the will, the steadfastness, the tenacity, they give in under the slightest struggle... Everyone says 'I wish I was in your shoes.' They don't know the tenth of it. If they were in my shoes, they would cry like a baby," said Mike. When Mike was asked about having critics, he would respond, "It doesn't matter what anyone says about me. Doesn't faze me what others say about me. I am a totally different entity of what others think of me."

Kai Greene *world-renowned body builder*

We spoke briefly about Kai Greene, a professional bodybuilder, earlier in this book. Additionally, his most recent victory was the Prague Pro in 2013. He was the first runner-up at the 2012 and 2013 Mr. Olympia competition. Kai comes from a humble beginning in Brooklyn, New York. He grew up in foster care and residential treatment centers. Throughout the years, Kai has become one of the most inspiring and motivational bodybuilders on the planet! So with great honor, I share his philosophy, work ethic and mindset for greatness with you.

The Mindset of Kai Greene

"The mind is everything. If you don't believe you can do something then you can't. It's like you have to save your own life. No one is going to save it for you. So we have to do what we have to do, no matter what it is," Kai said. His system of beliefs is intense and extreme to many. By the same token, it is necessary to have a similar system of beliefs when you are trying to reach the supreme level that many people fear to strive towards.

I watched an interview of Kai where he stated that there is a lot of thought required to be in touch with your inner champion. Wow! Your inner champion. How many of us know what he's talking about? We are already champions; we just have to match our work ethic and mindset with our true self. "You have great potential. But what will allow you to use that potential to see it fully realized is how important it is to you. Once you decide it's important to you, you will be able to use the necessary tools for you to win.".

This journey isn't built for everyone. There is a great amount of agony and pain you have to go through. "Just because it's harder for you to see your greatness, doesn't mean it's not there and true," said Kai. I always think about how many people came from the slums and against all odds became giants in their world. Kai, like many icons, believes nothing comes without sacrifice. "We all have to pay the price to be great in life," says Kai's coach. "Go through whatever hell to reach heaven," says Kai. He doesn't consider his training or path as suffering. He totally enjoys and loves what he does in bodybuilding. One of the statements I heard him say that reverberated to my core was, "You represent a whole other idea when you go to the next level."

Kai Greene Mindset

I can appreciate Kai's mindset. I was blown away not only by his enthusiasm for his beliefs, but also the intensity I felt when he talked about them. He believes that all great bodybuilders have to be great thinkers. He stated that there must be a focused concentration straight to the end. In order to achieve this, you have to be a great thinker. Just like his workouts and training, Kai embodied his thoughts when he stated that we have to have a certain type of desperation in order to become one with our passion.

"*Everything has an impact.*"

-Kai Greene's Philosophies

Kai states that people won't believe your methods until they see the visual results. Do you agree with this? Most people (especially men) are visual beings. You can talk about how you are going to accomplish your vision, dreams, goals, ideas, etc. but not until there is actual (physical) progress will people begin to gravitate towards you. Kai also states the following, "When a man embarks on a journey to achieving something that challenges their best or to bring forth their best (the best concentration, the best focuses of their thoughts), you will end up having to stop and think, Why am I doing this, because at times it can become overwhelming." This is true on so many levels. When you are pushing yourself to a higher place in your life, it will be physically and mentally draining. It will make you start to doubt yourself. You may start to feel like you are walking a tight-rope across a cliff and ask yourself, "Why am I doing this with no safety equipment? I must be out of my mind!" No support. No backup plan. How you respond to this emotion will determine your outcome.

"When you train to unleash your greatness, it's both your sanctuary and your prison," says Kai. You can train your mind to think differently than you have throughout the years, but it will be hell. It will be challenging, but then so rewarding. When we are in the trenches to self-development, being in a place you once loved (comfort) can easily become a place you hate (transformation). This is because we begin to realize that this place we know, this place we've grown accustomed to, has become a hindrance to our process. But this is normal because you go through many stages of development and all the emotions you experience are done under one roof. Kai goes on to speak about the spotlight. The same spotlight will be there when you succeed and it will be there when you don't. But this is what you asked for. We rise and fall on our path and it will more than likely happen in the spotlight of some sort because your transformation will grab many people's attention. Accept this and know that it comes with the territory. No need to be mad about it. Embrace it and let it keep you humble and grounded along the way.

Kai says that it all boils down to self-mastery. It's not about putting on a show or boosting our ego. We have an obligation to focus on what is most important: our practices and development.

Kai Greene's Work Ethic

Kai's work ethic is dynamic. It is unreal the capacity we have to push ourselves (mind, body, and spirit) to levels that can far exceed our expectations. Kai reads more books than watching television. (Television can be a detrimental distraction.) His reading list includes:

- *What Got You Here, Won't Get You There* - Marshall Goldsmith
- *The Science of Being Great* - Wallace D. Wattles
- *The Greatest Success in the World* - Og Mandino
- *As a Man Thinketh* - James Allen
- *Unlimited Power* - Tony Robbins
- *The Shift* - Wayne Dyer

Kai is very prepared and consistent with his workout and habits. He believes that warm-ups allow a person an opportunity to check in with themselves. It's the best time to start an internal dialog. "Hey, how am I doing? What am I about to do? Why is this important to me? Why am I here?" It's a meditative process to go inside yourself and talk to yourself. While training for the Mr. Olympia competition, Kai was on a very strict diet (and I don't mean just his eating habits.) There were no women, no television, and no idle time spent on nonsense. Every moment of the day was like a walking meditation for Kai and his trainer. He was completely focused on the end result.

When it's time for competition, Kai and his training team fly out to the location of the competition 7 weeks before the actual event. He disconnects himself from everyone and the environment he is accustomed to. This allows him to be away from any distractions and simply focus on the task at hand. I watched the documentary of Kai preparing for the Mr. Olympia competition. Here is what I found:

- The atmosphere where Kai and his trainer stayed was very somber and quiet
- No one spoke during dinner.
- During the entire stay, only motivational videos and church sermons played on the television. Only motivational CDs and DVDs played in the rooms and car.
- Kai was in a meditative state for 24 hours a day/ 7 days a week
- He would work out at various times of the day. He was never on a set schedule. Kai's schedule was NO SCHEDULE. (Sounds very familiar to Bruce Lee's philosophy, doesn't it?)
- He was working out at 12:00 midnight. He would do cardio at 3am for an hour and eat according to his needs.
- If he felt he wasn't ready to go to the gym, he would go back to bed.

Kai's training ritual is impressive and admirable. Kai stated that **we must create an oasis of discipline.** Daily, Kai sits in complete silence while his coach repeatedly chants positive affirmations in his ear. It is also a part of Kai's system of belief that we must master the art and discipline of repetition while maintaining a high level of self-motivation.

Michael Jackson *world-renowned music artist*

Michael Jackson was supreme in his work ethic and belief system as well. Michel will be forever be known as the King of Pop. This is because what he did behind the scenes and behind the stage, left a deep footprint of his greatness on the world. From my studies of Michel, here are some things that I found about him:

- Music wasn't just music to Michael. It was a legacy. While others did it for fun, he took it as seriously as if his life depended on it. Music for him was his reputation and a standard that he continually matched and went beyond. He had accomplished so much, so early in his career that he had no choice but to expand higher. THE KING OF POP.
- He believed thinking had no place when IN the moment. "Thinking is the biggest mistake a dancer can do. You have to feel," Michael once said.
- He believed that when the world told him no, he had to say yes.
- He believed that he had to be the physical embodiment of the music. He had to be the bass, clarinet, sax, drums, the entire orchestra. (This goes for anyone in any field. In order to succeed, you have to become the full embodiment of your craft.)

Michael was never satisfied with what he did. He always searched for ways to make what he did better. He would constantly be in the studio coming up with ideas and listening to music tracks. His producers and team considered them great tracks but Michael always felt they could be better. And once they did come up with something better than the last, Michael would see if it could be even better than that. Michael was the ultimate perfectionist with the highest of expectations and was always in competition with himself.

It was said that Michael would set his standard so high that he couldn't see himself losing. Michael would wake up in the early morning and would practice his routines nonstop for whatever concert was coming up. Michael would be on the stage at 3 am/4 am, practicing and performing. He would wake up the security guards and after awhile they became familiar with Michael early morning rituals.

Michael was never pleased with his performances. He always said that his next performance would be the toughest because he would have to try and outdo what he just did. He would review films of himself when he practiced in his free time. One of Michael's choreographers said, "We go through many, many, many levels of choreography, many looks and many types of approaches. But until it's the right thing, he doesn't stop and we don't stop either."

Michael worked harder than most. He would put in at least 12-hour days, sometimes 7 days a week. Even with this brutal work schedule, the dancers all agreed that it paid off. Michael kept a person at practice to take notes. Michael oversaw everything his team did. He said, "It's all about knowing what you want to do and having the will to do it."

When Michael and his team were creating the mini show, "Ghost," the choreographer stated that there was a tremendous amount of pressure. Michael was very demanding and not easily satisfied to the point where he would not allow his team of dancers, staff, etc. to leave any project imperfect. Michael's dancers would often choreograph a new set that they thought was very strong and cool.

Michael would watch, and then calmly ask, "Is this the absolute best you can do or it can be improved?" He strived for perfection and excellence and would settle for nothing less.

Oprah Winfrey *world-renowned media proprietor, talk show host, actress, producer, and philanthropist*

Another one of my studies included the awesome Oprah Winfrey. I always look at Oprah as Auntie O. You know, the aunt that you love because she keeps it real; she sees the best in you and always drops some awesome insight to help you bring it out. I smiled the entire time as I took notes of my Auntie O's life and career. I noticed the majority of what I read and watched was mostly in the tune of spiritual awakenings, the development of belief systems, and some power lines of wisdom that were passed along to her. I came to understand that with Oprah, because her belief system, faith and appreciation of her life, are all in harmony, greatness was her only destiny.

We Are All Beacons of Light

Oprah always admires and marvels at her life. She stated in an interview with Barbara Walters, "I marvel at the grace God has shown me." She has this sense of connecting to something higher than herself--she is God-fearing. She lives in the rawness of truth. She speaks in truth and accepts it for what it's worth. In having a mindset such as embracing and accepting raw truth, we can make honest decisions and recognize the truth about ourselves. Along with this, Oprah has a small, yet strong, circle of support in her life. She believes that you must surround yourself with people who can be honest to you, especially about you. Having this type of support system will help you be a brighter light in the world.

In 1998, Oprah received an Emmy Lifetime Achievement Award. During her speech, she spoke about how she prayed to God to use her. It was a resonating speech that I've watched several times over. It gives us a glimpse of her belief system and faith in her vision: "God, use me. Use me. Use this life. I don't know what the future holds for me, but I know there is a vision for my life that's greater than my imagination can hold. Use me. Use me. What would you have me do?" How powerful! She knows there is something greater for her and she allows herself to be open to whatever it is without hesitation. This is a belief that has been used by our past greats as well as our modern-day greats.

Oprah often talks about the greatness in surrendering all and how there was no better moment that she experienced the effect of it than when she was cast for the role in the movie, "The Color Purple." During an episode of her show Master Class (that is usually aired on her very own network), she said, "God can dream a bigger dream for me, for you, then you could ever dream for yourself. When you worked as hard, done as much, and strived, tried, and given, and pleaded, bargained, and hoped…Surrender. When you have done all that you could do, and there's nothing left for you to do, give it up to that thing that is greater than yourself and let it the become a part of the flow."

We can stand strong in our power to claim greatness into our lives. When Oprah was giving her speech, she said, "I want to continue to use television as we become more polarized in this medium. I choose to use it in whatever way I can, we can, to make people lead better lives. To lead them to the highest vision possible for themselves. That's the goal." Oprah's beliefs are something special. She goes on to say that what we believe to be true, is true for us. What we believe to be possible for us, will be possible for us. Her grandmother was a maid and her only real expectation for Oprah was that she too would become a maid. But Oprah, at a very young age, believed deep down in her heart, being a maid would not be her destiny. "Somewhere I have always known that I was born for greatness."

Over time, Oprah stated that because she sensed that something greater was in store for her life, she held onto that feeling for a very long time. No matter what strikes she had against her, she continued to believe that she was destined for something bigger, greater. "At different times in your life, the call will be different," says Oprah. "Many people ask about, 'What is my purpose? How am I supposed to know what I'm supposed to do?' The only way to know what to do in your life is to pay attention to the life you are living right now. You can't get it by listening to other people. You can't allow the voices of the world to drown out, that which I know, is the voice of God. The voice of your own consciousness. The voice of the purest light of yourself. That is how the energy of God speaks to all of us."

Oprah Words of Manifestation

"You will manifest the life that you believe. I always knew that no matter what my belief is, I'm going to be alright. Why? Because I have that faith of a mustard seed. I believe the people who are most successful and are able to handle that success in such a way that it fulfills them and don't overwhelm them are the people who understand that belief." She gives direct advice by saying, "Whatever you believe you were born to do, you do it. You find a way to allow the truth of yourself to express itself. Because that's what we're all looking for. The highest, fullest expression of ourselves as human beings."

60 Minutes Interview (1986)

In 1986, Oprah was interviewed on an American TV show called "60 Minutes." It was during the season that she would launch the Oprah Winfrey Show. As I watched the interview, I was blown away by what she was claiming and how what she stated in 1986 has come to reality today. Here are the words from her that left me in shock and awe: "I am where I am because I always believed I could get here. Always believed it." When she was asked about her show that was about to launch she stated, "It's going to do well." And when the host of the show followed up with the question, "If it doesn't?" Oprah quickly said, "If it doesn't, I will still do well. I will do well because I'm not defined by the show. We are defined by the way we treat ourselves and how well we treat other people. It would be wonderful to be acclaimed as this talk show host who made it. That would be wonderful. But if that doesn't happen, there are other important things in my life."

J.K. Rowling *world renowned author*

"If you choose to use your status and influence to raise your voice on behalf of those who have no voice; if you choose to identify not only with the powerful, but with the powerless; if you retain the ability to imagine yourself into the lives of those who do not have your advantages, then it will not only be your proud families who celebrate your existence, but thousands and millions of people whose reality you have helped change. We do not need magic to change the world, we carry all the power we need inside ourselves already: we have the power to imagine better." –J. K. Rowling

I could have never completed this book without sharing with you some of J.K. Rowling's insights and thoughts. J.K., author of the Harry Potter series, is another woman I admire. I enjoy listening to her interviews and her process of writing one of the most famous series ever. Throughout the years, I would take little notes of something she said that sparked the philosopher in me. I recognize that her work ethic is very different from those I shared with you in this book. But when it comes to her belief system and what she loves to do, there is no denying that she is one of the greats of our time.

J.K Rowling's Vision

J.K. states numerous times in interviews that she always knew there would be 7 books in her Harry Potter series. When asked about it she always knew that these books would be a success, she begins to tell about the voice that she heard in her head while writing her book "Harry Potter and The Sorcerer's Stone." She states that while writing she heard a voice say, "The difficult thing is to get published. If it get's published, it will be huge." We all can hear these voices that direct us clearly, but how often do we truly listen and obey? J.K. was denied 12 times by 12 different publishers, but remained determined to succeed. It took her 17 years to complete her amazing book series and even when her literary agent said, "You'll never make money writing children books," she continued to push forward.

When she was 25 years of age, J.K. was on a train that was delayed when the idea came to her about Harry Potter. She had no pen but still allowed her imagination to run free and acknowledge the space she was in. She was excited and knew that she had to get this on paper. This is what vision does to us when we are open to receive. We get excited and become completely consumed by the energy that the universe pours into us. As far back as J.K can remember, all she wanted to be is a published writer. Being a single-parent on welfare was not making that vision an easy process to accomplish. But still, J.K. kept pushing forward. She says it was her adrenaline that kept her moving forward to deal with the truth when she hit the lowest point of her life.

"Rock bottom was the solid foundation in which I rebuilt my life," says J.K. (Remember when we spoke about ruin being a gift?) She goes on to say, "Failure strips away the inessential...If I succeeded at anything else, I might have never had found the determination in the one arena that I truly believe I belonged...It is impossible to live and not fail at something. Unless you live so cautiously that you might have not lived at all. In which case, you failed by default." She believes failure is a great teacher and holds an oasis of wisdom for us all. "You will never truly know yourself or the strength of your relationships until both have been tested by adversity."

When you want to tap into your greatness, you have to be fully involved in all you do while you walk your path. J.K. loves writing books more than anything. Writing her Harry Potter books was her joy. It meant the world to her because she was given the experience of discipline and structure. It gave her life. She knew she would write more, but when it came to the last book of the Harry Potter series, she cried because she knew that particular story had to come to an end. This is a pure example of being truly involved in your journey and appreciating your talent.

Finding Our Sanctuaries

There was a day where it was very noisy at J.K,'s home and she couldn't work. She realized that she could solve the problem by leaving the environment to a quieter place. So she checked into a hotel. She ended up staying there to finish all of her Harry Potter books. Hearing her say this makes me think of how having a quiet room or a personal sanctuary can allow us to be completely in tune with God and the universe. We are able to sift through all the imaginary clutter and artificial noise. We are able to be at our best and do our best because we are in a place of quietness and stillness.

J.K. used her talent to the highest level possible with tenacity and discipline. She created something so great that her work and energy affected millions of people around the world. This will continue for generations to come. There is power in writing your vision down on paper. It begins to become an actuality. In J.K's first Harry Potter book, she wrote in one of the story lines, "One day every child in the world will know his name." How powerful is that line all by itself? She stated that if she had nothing else, she had confidence in her story.

J.K. loves every aspect of writing. She said that the moment she received that vision on the train at 25 years of age, she knew she was meant to write. "I know what I believe because of what I've written," she says. "We all have to decide what constitutes failure. The world is eager to give you a set of criteria if you let it."

J.K. Process of Work

Her writing process is simple but what is the most important is that she writes with complete focus and enjoyment. She makes her stories a part of her life in several ways. She made Harry's birthday the same as hers along with his economic status. She takes her time to weave in life pearls all throughout the book such as love, loyalty, trust, friendship, standing for what you believe, and standing up against negativity and evil.

When she finishes writing and the editor has completed their task, she goes back over every single page to tighten it up one last time. The book must be flawless in all ways. During the release of the final book, she did a midnight book release where everyone around the world would have to receive it all at the same time. She would also sign an estimated 2,000 books (8 hours worth of signing). I call that appreciation and hard work at the same time. When she finished the book, J.K. said something that I believe could not only be applied to her book, but to our lives as whole: "Some people won't be happy because what they wanted to happen hasn't happened." Yes, because we don't follow other people's vision of us, they might not like or condone what we do for the vision we see ourselves in. When it comes to our work, J.K. said, "For some people to love it; others must loathe it. That's just the nature of the plot."

Rahfeal Gordon's 21 Days of Greatness Journey Activity

Whenever I am dealing with inner conflict, I tend to get away from everything to focus on myself. The time I take away from everything to regroup can be anywhere from 7 days to 90 days. It truly works for me so I wanted to share this with you.

Any time you feel that you've lost your way or that you've outgrown your current level, take this 21-day journey to regroup and get yourself back on track. It's a simple way of cleaning out all the mess you collected along the way.

There is only one rule with this activity: There is NO RULE. I want you to constantly remind yourself that everything is already perfect. Constantly remind yourself that you are just getting back in harmony with your positive energy, greater vibration and a gaining a sharper view of your amazing vision.

Take each day as it comes. One day at a time. I usually give something up while doing this activity. Something that I know has been a distraction on my journey. I suggest only watching positive videos and listening to music that will stimulate your mind in a positive way. Enjoy your daily activities and may your brightest star shine through you. May your vision of greatness become your greatest reality.

How to Begin the 21-Day Journey

1. Read the message twice a day (once in the morning and once before bed).
2. Take 10-15 minutes to reflect on the message.
3. Keep the message fresh in your mind. Make it a point of discussion with others throughout the day.
4. In the evening, reflect on the message and see how it played a part in your day.
5. **Remember:** The goal of these activities is to get your mind back in alignment with your vision. It is meant to have you sift through and purge any mental and physical clutter that may be hindering you in moving forward.

Day # 1 of 21 Days of Greatness Journey

The Focus: FORGIVENESS

Today is about forgiveness. Many of you have some awesome dreams and goals that you want to achieve. You have been trying for weeks, months, and even years but have had no major progress in development to bring you closer to reaching them. I would like to suggest taking a u-turn and ride down the path of forgiveness. Forgiveness is powerful and a very important tool for all of us. When we forgive, we are releasing our internal grips from past emotions, mistakes and problems. We are saying to God, "Hey God, just so you know, I'm letting go. Please take over now." This creates room for new things (blessings) in your life. You give your attention to what's actually happening in your life presently (not what "didn't happen" or "had happened" in your life). When we don't forgive, we continue to hold onto past experiences that hinder us for enjoying our gifts of the present. You could be judging your present situations (business partners, new relationships, and experiences) based on the things you didn't forgive in your past. Maybe you haven't forgiven yourself for past mistakes and that is the reason your belief system of who you are isn't matching your goals and dreams. Forgive those who hurt you. Forgive yourself for the mistakes you made. Forgive, even if others will not forgive you. We've all made mistakes with the best intentions in mind. Forgive your parents for not being there. Forgive your neighbors for not helping protect the kids in the community. Forgive the people that hurt you in previous relationships. You can't get what you truly yearn until you clean that rundown shack of old feelings, aggression, hate, and negative energy. Make room for the blessings that are on their way. Start your forgiveness process today! Look in the mirror and forgive yourself. Make some phone calls. Set up some one-on-one time with close relatives and friends. Knock it out today. Stop waiting. Your greatness awaits you! Start with forgiveness. Start with being healed.

Day # 2 of 21 Days of Greatness Journey

The Focus: CLEAR VISION

Oftentimes, when we set our short-term goals, we make to-do lists. We visualize the finish line (outcome) and then begin to write down what we think will be the best paths (goals and steps) to make it happen. To achieve our vision, we should do the same. Visualize the finish line and create a to-do list. With this to-do list, however, we must make sure to be crystal clear down to the smallest detail. If your vision is to be a doctor, what medical school will you go to? What type of doctor will you be? What facility will you work in? Likewise, if your vision is to inspire the world, in what manner will you inspire them? In what capacity will you inspire them? What will you inspire them to do? When we have a crystal clear vision, we begin to truly recognize which opportunities are great for us.

As you continue to embark on your journey towards your greatness, you will come across (and attract) all types of amazing opportunities. But you must remember that every amazing opportunity will not be amazing *for you*. If your vision is to travel more, you should not be accepting opportunities that will keep you stagnant in your current location. If your vision is to be debt-free, you should not be buying concert tickets with your friends to see your favorite artists perform just because you (currently) have the money in the bank to do so. Think of it like this, when you are debt-free, getting VIP tickets to see your favorite artist perform will be your new normal. That is having VISION!

Here is what I want you to do today. Write out a 1-2 line statement of what you want to accomplish by December 31st of this year. I want you to be crystal clear. Let's say you wanted to raise funds for a start-up organization, you need to establish an exact amount. "I AM going to save $5,000 by December 31st of this year to use as start-up money for the global non-profit organization I want to establish. My global organization will provide school children of impoverished areas with school supplies throughout the entire school year." Our visions are powerful. The actions behind them are even more powerful. Act accordingly.

Day # 3 of 21 Days of Greatness Journey

The Focus: WORK ETHIC

If our visions were considered words, then our work ethic would define them. Work ethic by definition is a value based on hard work and diligence. It is also a belief in the moral benefit of work and its ability to enhance the character. When you are striving to make your vision(s) a reality, your work ethic will define how valuable and important those visions are to you. What time do you arrive to work? 15-30 minutes early or 15-30 minutes late? How many hours do you put aside for personal development? How many books have you read to help you achieve your vision since the New Year began? Be honest. Are you truly giving your all to achieve your greatest self? Michael Jackson woke up at 3am-4am almost daily to rehearse and perfect his concert routines. Kobe Bryant would not leave any of his practices before shooting 400 jump shots. Mike Tyson woke up at 4:00am faithfully to run a few miles because he believed that would give him a sharper competitive edge over his opponents.

Take the time to review your calendar and actions for the next few weeks. Where are you spending your daily 1,440 minutes? Tighten up your arrival time to all activities. Work extra hard to master your weaknesses. Learn from those who have or are currently dominating the arenas in which they are a part of. You have to make some hard core sacrifices if you want to attain greatness. Greatness cannot be attained by just a 9-5 work ethic. You have to go above and beyond what is normal and average. Your visions are supreme. So should your work ethic be. To whom much is given, much is required.

Day # 4 of 21 Days of Greatness Journey

The Focus: BE THE GARDENER

It's not about what is happening, it's about how you show up to what is happening. Each day you wake up, you are waking up in your garden. If you want to attain and unleash your greatness in the world, you must be a gardener every day of your life. If you choose otherwise, someone could take your position and plant bad seeds in your garden. The roots from those seeds could end up growing and destroying your beautiful garden. You have to clean your garden every day because people will try to litter it with lies and deceit. You have to protect it so that you are able to live off the fruits and vegetables that will grow from your garden.

We must take the responsibility of being great gardeners every day. We must do what needs to be done, not for the limelight, but for our own personal fulfillment and to be great servants of the world. We must recognize the weeds in our garden and get rid of them immediately. When we take care of our gardens, we can feed the masses with our fruits and vegetables (knowledge and wisdom). We can experience true joy and share the process of what we did to grow it. Great gardeners prune their gardens however they want and not by the instruction of others. They work hard in their gardens so that they have more than enough during their harvest season.

Be the gardener of your greatness. "Those who work their land will have abundant food, but those who chase fantasies will have their fill of poverty. A faithful person will be richly blessed, but one eager to get rich will not go unpunished." - Proverbs 28:19-20

Day # 5 of 21 Days of Greatness Journey

The Focus: INspire

Inspired by definition means, "outstanding or brilliant in a way, or to a degree suggestive of divine inspiration." On the road to our greatness, we will encounter some heavy storms and heartaches. But we must always remind ourselves why we are on this journey. We have to constantly push ourselves to walk down the road that we are never completely prepared for. Greatness isn't for the weak or the insecure. Greatness is not for people who are inspired only by what's happening on the outside. Greatness is for those who are INspired from the INside. It is for those that want to transcend their talent and gift to inspire others withIN their world. It is the divine way to be like this. INspiration starts with the two letters "IN" for a reason. It signifies that withIN you is the energy necessary to keep you moving steady towards your greatness. Someone once asked me how they could be an inspiration. My reply was, "Simply by being you." There is no other person in the world like you. There are billions of people in the world and yet, you were uniquely created to be the reflection of the greatest source of energy known to man. So you must first, recognize and accept this. Then, with this knowledge, walk IN all your glory. You must love your life and do whatever makes you happy and stay INspired.

Day # 6 of 21 Days of Greatness Journey

The Focus: SELF-ACCEPTANCE

The achievement of your greatness and genuine happiness will never be possible until you gain some degree of self-acceptance. The most miserable and tortured people in the world are those who are continually straining and striving to convince themselves and others that they are something other than what they are. There is no relief or satisfaction like when a person finally gives up the shams and pretenses and is willing to be him/herself. Changing your self-image does not mean changing "yourself"; it means changing your own mental picture, your own estimation and conception of yourself. You are what you are NOW. Most of you are better, wiser, stronger, more competent NOW, at this very moment, than you realize. You are more than a "somebody". After all, God created you in his own image. Having material things might make you "somebody" to people. But remember, you are not who people say you are. You are what God says that you are.

Self-acceptance means accepting and coming to terms with ourselves now, just as we are, with all our faults, weaknesses, shortcomings, errors, as well as our assets and strength. Self-acceptance is easier, however, if we realize that these negative things do not have to belong to us. Many people shy away from healthy self-acceptance because they insist on identifying themselves with their mistakes. Just because you made a mistake, doesn't mean you are that mistake. We must recognize our mistakes and shortcomings before we correct them.

The first step toward acquiring knowledge is in recognizing those areas where we are ignorant. The first step towards becoming stronger is the recognition that we are weak. As we continue down our journey to our greatness, we must achieve our goal of self-acceptance. We must use the negative feed-back data to correct our course, not steer it.

Day # 7 of 21 Days of Greatness Journey

The Focus: SURRENDER

Surrender means you are willing to accept that God is active in your life, whether or not you can see Him working. When you surrender, you are no longer attached to the labels and the opinions that people put on your life. You are completely giving yourself to the universal laws that make mountains tall, water flows, and children smile just *because*. One of the biggest challenges people face in life is their willingness, strength, and discipline to change by surrendering. All that we are able to accomplish in life will be determined by our understanding of how life works. It doesn't matter how fast, how hard, or with how much bravado you live. When we surrender our all, we move to a higher awareness, acknowledgement, acceptance, and understanding of how life flows. That will determine how and where you live in the universal scheme of things.

We are all made imperfectly perfect in order to fulfill our purpose perfectly. When you surrender you begin to realize that every step you take, every mistake you've made, every pain you've experienced, every moment of happiness you were a part of, and every thought you acknowledged was and will always be perfect.

Make it a daily ritual to surrender yourself to the universe and not to the demands of society. Remember you are a reflection of the most high and within you is the universe you are currently experiencing. No need for an identity crisis.

Day # 8 of 21 Days of Greatness Journey

The Focus: BE A REBEL WITH A CAUSE

Nothing/No one great will always stand with the crowd. When you are trying to attain something beyond the capacity of what others can envision, you will have to stand alone most of the time. When you make a decision to give everything you have towards your vision, you automatically become a rebel with a powerful cause. Your vision has to be so powerful that when achieved, it affects you and everyone connected to you. Rebels of greatness tend to be considered crazy at times (HA! Myself included.) and this is okay. Rebels of greatness are considered weird sometimes. And this is okay. Rebels of greatness will at some point have to deal with public and private hate at times. And this is okay. This is okay because they are built for it. They know that the end result of what they are trying to achieve is far greater than any personal opinion or negative comment mentioned about them. Rebels are the changing agents of the world. They shift individuals, communities, towns, cities, states, countries, continents, and the world.

Today make the decision to be content with being a rebel of greatness. Don't be afraid to break the rules to establish your foundation of greatness. Abide by the laws of the universe so that you can experience what true freedom is today. Live in your greatness no matter what your haters or naysayers think. Every rebel of greatness has favor over their life. You can be the change people need to see so that they can be liberated from their own burdens. Every great and iconic person that has tattooed their name in history has been a true rebel of greatness. Come with me through this journey of greatness as a rebel with a powerful cause. You can experience something different, walk taller, and think higher down this road. Trust me, there are some amazing rebels you would love to meet.

Day # 9 of 21 Days of Greatness Journey

The Focus: LIVE LIFE ON THE EDGE

Many people work extremely hard and never take advantage of the life they worked so hard for. To me, the people who are considered the failures are not only the ones that never took advantage of their blessings, but also the ones who never realized they made it to the top of their mountain. As you all continue to embark on your journey, make sure you live life to the fullest along the way. LIVE ON THE EDGE! Take advantage of life and all its wonders of the world. Don't sit around on a local level. Get your butt up and travel to lands that are foreign to you. Make those foreign lands your hang out spots. Make the world your playground. Always think and move on a global level. Creating music isn't the only way to live like a rock star.

Jump out of a plane. Have wine and dinner in a hot air balloon. Go skydiving. Go run in a marathon. Take a weekend trip to Paris. Pay for a stranger's meal and watch their reaction when they find out the bill has already been paid. Buy a group of kids some ice cream and tell them to follow you on Instagram just because you're cool. Go ahead and act like James Bond or Cleopatra for a day. Just LIVE ON THE EDGE and be an exciting person to hang around! Many people work extremely hard but are as shallow as puddles. This is because they don't open themselves up to the world. They don't allow their imagination to run free so that it can pull them in front of some of the most beautiful landscapes known to man.

LIVE ON THE EDGE. Be a bad boy with a good heart. Be a woman who is sassy yet classy. Live a little. When you are walking down your path that leads to greatness, you will accumulate some amazing experiences and tools to make a better life for yourself. Don't let these tools go to waste. You will be old one day and have to live with the regrets of not doing what you could have done today. Work hard, play hard. It's a golden rule for those who are tapping into their greatness.

Day #10 of 21 Days of Greatness Journey

The Focus: NEVER GO ON SALE

Let's get this straight from the start. Your life is valuable. This means your thoughts are valuable. This means your visions are valuable. This means everything you say and create in this world has value. This is why you should never settle for less in anything you do. When you know who you are and the destination you are trying to reach, why would you bargain for less? Honestly, why would you waste your time bargaining in the first place? Take a lesson from many of the high-end fashion designers such as Louis Vuitton, Gucci, and Valentino. Before the recession, during the recession, and after the recession (even to this day), you've never seen them lower their prices on any of their clothing, shoes, and accessories. You don't see commercials on TV promoting "one-day sales," holiday specials, or even see a sale rack in their stores. Why? Because they know the value of their company and the value of their vision. They know the value of their target clients. These designers know that their fashion designs, visions, and who they associate with are too valuable to be watered down for people who don't respect their value, their material, the time and effort they put into creating their products.

So use this as an example for your own life. Never lower your standards or put your vision up for sale. Don't accept or agree to things that belittle your value. You deserve the best out of life and you need to make sure you are treated with high regards. If other people want or allow others to treat their life as the 80% off final sale rack, then that's their decision. You have to understand that there are many people who are content with buying and stunting with the fake rather than buying and dealing with the real. Not everyone deserves your valuable time and attention (especially if you are making major moves on your journey). People will treat you cheap if you let them. If they don't treat their lives with respect, what makes you think they would treat yours as such? Remember: your life, your vision, your time and your attention isn't cheap. Don't hand out coupons and never, EVER give yourself up for sale.

Day #11 of 21 Days of Greatness Journey

The Focus: HAVE A SENSE OF HUMOR

How boring is a person who works all day to achieve their personal greatness with no sense of humor? VERY BORING. Learn to develop a great sense of humor along your journey. Laughter is inviting. You will attract more friends and even turn enemies into allies. It is a great character to have when the going gets tough as well. Those who have tapped into their personal greatness knows that we must laugh at the Goliaths we will come up against to show that no matter how difficult the battle may seem - we have no need to stress about it.

Having a sense of humor makes the journey to greatness more enjoyable. It helps us get through the toughest and the darkest of times in our lives. Having a sense of humor allows people to feel comfortable around you. They won't mind letting their guard down so that you can see their authenticity. We all need someone to get us through the long workloads with a little encouragement and laughter. Be that person. Life here on this earth isn't forever so we must try our best to make the most out of it; whether it's with a few great jokes or a few great laughs.

Day #12 of 21 Days of Greatness Journey

The Focus: BE A STUDENT OF LIFE

We all must be students when it comes to life as a whole. If you want to live life to the fullest, you must first be the student that learns how to live. A student by definition is a person who is studying at school or college. They take an interest in a particular subject. Well, we must allow life to be our school and make living our subject of interest. We must be willing to be open to allowing every person and experience that we encounter to be our teachers in the school of life. As students, it's very important to be open to learning various methods and ways of living so that we are truly prepared for whatever test we receive in the school of life.

Our journey towards greatness can be a beautiful learning experience if we decide to be lifelong students. We must master the art of living so that we will be able to share our methods and experiences with others. When we first embarked on our journey, we automatically became a blueprint for someone who is looking for the motivation to embark on their own journey. Because of this, we must strive to be great students so that these individuals can see that the first rule to being a great teacher in life is to first be a great student. Make it a standard to be a great student today so that you not only be one of the best blueprints in life, but also so you can reach the top of life's classes.

Day #13 of 21 Days of Greatness Journey

The Focus: SPEAK OVER YOUR LIFE

Who told you this morning that you were beautiful? Who tells you that you are amazing every day? Who tells you everything will be okay and to keep pushing when it seems nothing is going right? Your first answer should always be you. Our journey to greatness is as long as it is constant. So we must always be able to speak over our lives words of encouragement and prosperity. When you constantly speak over your life, things will begin to manifest in your life. Words are powerful. Especially when you use them as a tool to build up your life. Prepare an uplifting statement for yourself like, "Today I am the summer that people yearn for in the winter." "Every day I will wake up in purpose and make my life an example of joy." "This outfit looks amazing on this body of mine. I am going to have to keep some neck braces in my car just for the people who are going to break their neck to get a glimpse of this amazing situation." (I actually know some awesome people with great mindsets like this.).

Our journey to personal greatness will be whatever we speak it to be. Some may speak of their journey as if it's a catwalk in a major fashion show. Others may speak of it as walking along the coast with their feet in white sands. We must always speak greatness, love, joy, and prosperity over our lives. Dr. Maya Angelou once said, "Words are things. One day we will be able to measure the power of words." I believe we can already measure them. All we have to do is listen to the words people say and observe the actions within their lives. What have you been speaking lately?

Day #14 of 21 Days of Greatness Journey

The Focus: Carry a Hammer and Sword

Listen to me carefully. When you are on your journey or path towards greatness, you must carry a hammer and sword at all times. Why? Because the hammer is what you use to build foundations and a sword is what you use to protect it. It symbolizes the foundation of your self-esteem, confidence, character, goals and dreams. Many people (some strangers and some close ties) will try to take and/or destroy the foundations you've built along your journey. Use your sword to protect it. The sword symbolizes strength, courage, fearless, and inner power. It's what we all need to carry when we walk down this path that will test us to our very core.

Nothing you've created or are connected to should be treated with a lack of value or respect. Keep your sword sharp at all times (fear nothing). Protect your goals and dreams at all costs. Protect the personal foundations you've created that helped build your faith, self-esteem, confidence, and a sense of appreciation for the life you live. Build a strong foundation with your hammer (insight/knowledge/experiences/advisors) and preserve it at all costs with your sword. As long as you have one in each hand, your territory will forever expand. Be Great!

Day #15 of 21 Days of Greatness Journey

The Focus: KEEP YOUR CIRCLE IN SHAPE

How strong is your circle? You must have people in your circle that are strong in various areas. You need mentors, advisors, true friends and supportive family members while on your journey towards greatness. These individuals must be able to stand strong in their spot with and without you. They are self-disciplined, self-motivated, intelligent, and push you towards your greatness. Weak people cannot be allowed in your circle. You can't have leeches in your circle. You can't have gossipers in your circle. You can't have people who focus on others rather than themselves in your circle. You can't have people who don't know themselves in your circle.

You are trying to achieve GREATNESS and you MUST have wise advisors in your circle. I am a big fan of the Book of Proverbs in the Bible. One of my favorite verses is, "Plans go wrong for lack of advice; many advisers bring success" (Proverbs 15:22). You need people who are going to put you in your place in private, so that you don't embarrass yourself in public. They want the best for you. They are your strength in your areas of weakness. They see your visions and know it as if it were their own. Don't get it twisted; they will help guide you down your path but they won't walk it for you. They simply have the best advice, wisdom, knowledge, and support you need to get you through the journey! Know the body of your circle and keep it in shape!

Day #16 of 21 Days of Greatness Journey

The Focus: BE STILL AND CALM YOUR CHAOS

As we all know, chaos can come in all forms in our lives. One of the most extreme forms of chaos we can encounter is the one we create within ourselves. Chaos means complete disorder and confusion. They say it's a behavior so unpredictable that it would appear to be random, owing to great sensitivity to small changes in conditions. Chaotic systems are predictable for a while and then "appear" to become random.

Quite interesting, right? The time frame for which the behavior of a chaotic system can be predicted depends on three things: How much uncertainty we are willing to tolerate in the forecast; the accuracy of which we are able to measure its current state; a time scale depending on the dynamics of the system.

When we believe we are having a chaotic moment on our journey, it's our own belief system that confirms this. Sometimes people will adopt someone else's chaos as their own. As a result, they tend to stress about a chaotic moment they didn't create. When we are having a moment due to overwhelming of assignments, responsibilities, family problems, or unorganized situations – just step back and BE STILL.

Recognize that you are in control and can calm the situation. Power and Peace dwell in the individuals who can create it in the middle of their chaos. When you can own your chaos, then you can measure it and decide how much of it you will tolerate. Finally, you will be able to calm it.

Day #17 of 21 Days of Greatness Journey

The Focus: ALWAYS KNOW THE FACTS

A fact is knowledge or information based on real occurrences. It is also something demonstrated to exist or known to have existed. Be aware of how you digest information given to you by others. Many people get their source of information from television while others may get their source of information from those closest to them. Even though we may have a certain amount of trust with these individuals and media outlets, we must still verify the information we allow ourselves to be fed.

As you continue your journey towards greatness, you don't want to fall due to false information that someone else gave you. You want facts only. When a person gives you information, don't be afraid to question its source. Be sure to question the things you read in books, the things you hear on the radio, and the things you see on television. You want to make decisions, whether big or small, based upon FACTS ONLY. Not assumptions. Not opinions. And definitely not maybes. When you make decisions based upon the facts, you will see great things happen while on your journey.

Day #18 of 21 Days of Greatness Journey

The Focus: NEVER HESITATE

Gandhi once said, "Men often hesitate to a beginning because they feel that the objective cannot be achieved in its entirety. This attitude of mind is precisely our greatest obstacle to progress. An obstacle that each man, if he only will it, clear away." The journey is crowded with opportunities for you to develop and find your true self. It is scarcely populated with people who are fearful of what may happen in their lives. Hesitation is the action a person creates when they lack faith and ask God for the same thing over and over again. Their hesitation lies behind a repeated prayer knowing that the thing they have asked for will require their dedication and hard work as well. If they had supreme faith, they would ask only once (knowing HE knew their prayer before they prayed it) and spend the rest of the time working through the obstacles with extreme tenacity to reach their blessing.

Are you hesitating? Are you afraid of the blessing you are imagining could be around the corner? Just so you are reminded, the term "imagine" means to form a mental image or concept of; to suppose or assume. Again, hesitation comes from fear, lack of faith, and the lack of information to make a personal decision.

At this point, in Day #18, you have received 17 different tools to help build your faith, confidence and insight to walk without hesitation. Get to the root of your hesitation so that you can stand firm in the decisions you make on your journey. You got this! There is no time to hesitate because you have an appointment with greatness. And you can't be late!

Day #19 of 21 Days of Greatness Journey

The focus: BE THANKFUL

We must be thankful for the opportunity that we have been given in each second of our lives. We have to be thankful for waking up and being able to have the freedom to become great. What good is it to be on a journey that you are not thankful for? When you don't acknowledge how far you've come on your journey, you may begin to curse the steps you have taken. You may mistakenly look at all of your blessings as having no value. And this is not what people of greatness do. We, the people of greatness, look at every detail as being tailor-made just for us. And that is *everything* to be thankful for. Remember when you fell last week? You should be thankful for that. Why? Because there was a lesson in that fall and it was a custom-made lesson just for you.

A few years ago, Oprah said in an interview, "You can't be friends with someone who wants your life." She meant that each blessing is a personalized God-given gift. It is meant for you and you alone. These individuals aren't built to appreciate the blessings that you are to receive. If only for that, we must say thank you as much as we can each day. Thank you for this food, this eyesight to see beauty, this brain for my intelligence, my friends for support, this roof over my head, the blessing to know that of all the billions of people in the world – there is only one me. Be thankful along your journey and watch what happens along the way.

Day #20 of 21 Days of Greatness Journey

The Focus: CHANGE YOUR LANGUAGE

As you continue on your journey, you will eventually have to know the language of the world and universe. What I mean is that at a certain point, you will have to give up the ordinary talk about nothingness. You cannot be on a journey that has been established for kings and queens and yet you speak with a peasant tongue. You will never get far on your journey speaking the language of (mental) poverty.

Language is a method of human communication either spoken or written, consisting of the use of words in a structured and conventional way. It is a system of communication used by a particular community or country. Human language has the properties of productivity, recursivity, and displacement, and relies entirely on social convention and learning. This means, the group you socialize with has a direct affect on your language development.

What type of people do you socialize with? Leaders or weekly nightclub-goers? Investors or spenders? Where do you spend your time when you socialize? Do you spend it with individuals who don't appreciate their environment (or themselves) or at dinner parties with great global leaders? If you want to be great, spend your time amongst the great.

When you want to learn and speak the language of greatness, you listen and observe the great. It doesn't matter the distance to get to the lands where the great dwell. It doesn't matter how long it will take to get there. It doesn't matter if you are told that the language isn't spoken by the masses. Just go, learn, and speak the language of greatness. Because many are called, but few are chosen.

Day #21 of 21 Days of Greatness Journey

The Focus: STOP PRETENDING THAT YOU'RE NOT GREAT

Here we are at Day 21. I stayed committed every single day to pour into you. You now have 21 different tools to destroy the chains that hold you back from being your own master in life. You can now stop pretending that you are not great. You can stop dealing in those circles that believe they are going forward but are doing nothing but chasing their tails like a stray dogs.

Today is the day you wake up. To know thyself. To know that you are everything and everything is you. You have the power to change the view of the world and the power to change your inner world. Each person you meet in your lifetime is their own world. They all see the journey differently because they all (including yourself) have experienced life differently. Everything outside of you is your universe. You have the power to choose who will be your sun, moon, stars, and the planets that will be a part of your solar system.

On this journey, we must see our vision clearly and grow continuously because the essence of life is growth. If we do not grow, we do not live. And if we do not live, we will never know the full beauty of our lives. We are all creators. Everything you see in this world was created by someone who tapped into their greatness. The utensils you use to eat. The music you listen to during the day. The device you hold in your hand. This book I created for you. All of this, all of everything, originated from someone who made the decision to unleash their greatness.

We are all creators and when you decided to walk down this path of greatness, you made a promise to yourself to be one of the many great creators that have walked this planet. So today, stop pretending to be great and just BE GREAT. I pray that you continue to walk in light and love while on this amazing journey. It's never too late to leave your footprints on the path of greatness.

Thank you for reading this book in its entirety.

I wish you more love and light as you continue along your journey in this lifetime

Health & Wealth My Friend.

- Rahfeal Gordon

Book RahGor for Your Next Event

US Office: + 1 646. 358.4966
Fax: 646.358.4878
Website: www.RahGor.com

For All Speaking Appearances and Bulk Book Purchasing: **management@rahgor.com**
For All Media Attention: **publicrelations@rahgor.com**
For All Other Inquires: **info@rahgor.com**

Stay in Contact with RahGor on These Social Media Sites
LinkedIn Search: **Rahfeal Gordon**
Twitter and Instagram: **@RahGor**
Facebook: **www.facebook.com/rahfeal.gordon**

CPSIA information can be obtained
at www.ICGtesting.com
Printed in the USA
FFHW021444160519
52451926-57905FF